GW00599421

FIERCE THE CONFLICT

鬥爭的兇惡

Other titles by Norman Cliff

Courtyard of the Happy Way
Hijacked on the Huangpu
Captive in Formosa
A Flame of Sacred Love
The White Cliffs of Hangzhou
Prisoners of the Samurai

FIERCE *the* CONFLICT

by NORMAN H. CLIFF

鬥爭的兇惡

press

Dundas, Ontario

Joshua Press Inc., Dundas, Ontario, Canada
fax 905.627.8451 www.joshuapress.com

© 2001 by Joshua Press Inc.

All rights reserved. This book may not be reproduced, in whole or in part, without written permission from the publishers. Published 2001
Printed in Canada

Editorial director: Michael A.G. Haykin
Creative/production manager: Janice Van Eck

© Cover & book design by Janice Van Eck

National Library of Canada Cataloguing in Publication Data

Cliff, Norman H. (Norman Howard), 1925–
   Fierce the conflict (Dou zheng de xiong en)

Includes bibliographical references.

ISBN 1-894400-12-7

1. Christian biography—China. 2. Christianity—China—History—20th century.
3. China—Church history—20th century. I. Title. II. Title: Dou zheng de xiong en.

BR1296.C55 2001   275.1'082'0922   C2001–900935–6

This book is dedicated to my wife Joyce,
whose help and encouragement made
the writing of this book possible

Fierce may be the conflict,
Strong may be the foe...

In the service royal
Let us not grow cold;
Let us be right loyal,
Noble, true and bold.

Frances Ridley Havergal (1836–1879)
—from "Who is on the Lord's side?"

The Church is not fighting a conflict the issue of which is uncertain. The victory has been won, and therefore it must be won. The battle often thickens and presses upon the weary soldiers of the King, but they are but conflicts of administration. There is no question as to the final issue.

G. Campbell Morgan

They loved their Lord so good and dear,
  And His love has made them strong,
And they followed the right for Jesus' sake,
  The whole of their good lives long.
And one was a soldier, and one was a priest,
  And one was slain by a fierce wild beast;
And there's not any reason, no, not the least
  Why I shouldn't be a saint too.

They lived not only in ages past,
  There are hundreds of thousands still.
The world is bright with the joyous saints
  Who love to do God's will.
You can meet them in school, or in lanes, or at sea,
  In church, or in trains, or in shops, or at tea,
For the saints of God began just like me,
  And I mean to be one too.

L. Scott

CONTENTS

FOREWORD

—by Tony Lambert

This is an important book. As we stand at the beginning of the twenty-first century what do Christians see? With some exceptions, vibrant Christian faith is in decline in the West. The torch of biblical faith has been handed on to Third World countries in Africa, South America and Asia. Surprisingly, mainland China is rapidly becoming the front-runner worldwide in the number of evangelical Christians within its borders.

Recently an important Religious Affairs conference was held in Beijing. According to a report published in Hong Kong, the Chinese government admitted privately at that meeting that there are 25 to 35 million Protestant Christians in China. Publicly the figure issued by the Three Self Patriotic Movement has reached 15 million. If unregistered house church Christians are added, then it is quite possible that there are over 50 million Protestants in China, as well as 10 to 12 million Roman Catholics.

The total number of Christians thus now rivals the number of Party members, and is causing concern in high places. The "crisis of faith" (in Marxism) is widely acknowledged, as is the extent of "Christianity fever." However, the latter is no longer just affecting peasants in rural backwaters. Students, graduates, doctors, engineers and even Party cadres are becoming committed Christians. A leaked Party document from Guizhou admitted a few years ago that in one small area of that province some 2,000 Communist Party cadres had become Christians and some were openly serving as church elders. Last year I visited a large urban church in northeast China and interviewed one of the pastors, who told me that the total baptized membership of this one church is 20,000. Annually they baptize 1,000 new Christians. House church leaders in many regions also regularly baptize 200 to 300 new converts at a time.

Only twenty-five years ago it would have been quite unthinkable to imagine in one's wildest dreams that the Chinese church would not only survive, but multiply many times over. Most Western observers concluded that the Chinese church had been driven to the point of extinction by Maoism. Between 1966 and 1979 all churches in China were closed. Indeed, most had been closed by 1958. The harried and persecuted remnant of believers went underground.

Today that persecuted remnant has grown into a flourishing church. Today, if we take the lower estimate of 15 million, the Chinese church has grown twentyfold. If the higher, then over fiftyfold. This growth has all taken place over the last three decades since the closing years of the Cultural Revolution. We in the West can only look on with awe and amazement at the sovereign work of God.

But it is when we ask "Why China?" that we find Dr. Norman Cliff's book so valuable. Chinese and Western sociologists and researchers have come up with many theories, some no doubt valid. But few have looked back to the dark days of the fifties and sixties with spiritual discernment. As we read this book we are led to see that it was out of the crucible of persecution and severe testing of a handful of men and women of faith that God did a deep heart-work that laid the groundwork for the revival to come. Christ crucified was, and is, the centre of the faith of Chinese Christians. Walking the way of the cross they entered deeply into the fellowship of Christ's sufferings and emerged quietly triumphant.

This book further sheds light on the Chinese church during a grim period about which it is extremely difficult to acquire reliable information. In the secular field such biographies as *Wild Swans* and other first-hand accounts have graphically chronicled the collective madness of the Maoist years. In China it is now politically acceptable to admit the devastation caused the church by the Cultural Revolution (1966–1976). But a veil is still discreetly drawn over the severe testing of God's people that began in the early fifties. Overseas the names of Wang Mingdao and Watchman Nee are known and honoured as servants of God who suffered for their faith in China. But countless others are totally unknown. It is fitting that in this book some more of God's choice servants should now have their story told. Three of them are known personally to me. It has been a humbling and challenging experience to learn more of the Christian pilgrimage of our Chinese brothers and sisters.

May it be so for every reader.

Tony Lambert
Director for Research, Chinese Ministries,
OMF International

INTRODUCTION

In the course of my visits to China I have met some wonderful Christians. As they modestly told me their stories of all that they had been through I felt that I was sitting at the feet of some of God's saints.

This book is largely the fruit of these personal interviews, as well as of conversations with their families. These I have acknowledged at the end of this book together with those who have kindly assisted in the translation of letters and documents. My son James has assisted me greatly with the problems of using a computer, and has ensured that everything has been set out correctly. For any errors in this book I am solely responsible.

In putting these stories together I have a desire to share them with fellow Christians in the West, who have known so little about having to suffer for their faith.

These stalwarts of the church in China have fought the good fight of faith during the difficult years of the second half of the twentieth century. They come from different backgrounds and have worked in different provinces. Some have passed on to their reward, while the others, in spite of advancing years, are still serving God within their strength. One of the two whom I have not met is Watchman Nee (Ni Tuosheng), though I feel as though I have, having written a thesis about him some years ago. I have added further information about Nee and his wife, Charity Zhang (Zhang Pinhui), which I have learned subsequently.

Why have I chosen the title *Fierce the Conflict* for this book? There are many passages in the Bible which describe the Christian life as a constant warfare between God's people and the powers of evil. Paul says in Ephesians 6:12:

We are up against the unseen power that controls this dark world, and spiritual agents from the very headquarters of evil. (J.B. PHILLIPS)

The Lausanne International Congress on World Evangelisation, which met in 1974, made the following bold statement about spiritual warfare:

We believe that we are engaged in constant spiritual warfare with the principalities and powers of evil, who are seeking to overthrow the Church and frustrate its task of evangelization. We know our need to equip ourselves with God's armour, and to fight this battle with the spiritual weapons of truth and prayer.[1]

This book is about some Chinese Christians for whom conflict with the powers of evil was inevitable. Rather than conform to the exacting demands of a totalitarian and atheistic regime, they sought to continue witnessing for Christ, even though it meant adapting their style to a new situation.

This spiritual conflict is not confined to China. Principalities and powers have invaded the structures of our Western society. We need to recover our spiritual awareness of this phenomenon. As Michael Green states about Christianity in our society:

Church is only a place to go to once a week—or once a month—not a corps of battle troops under a Commander against a skilful, powerful and ruthless foe.[2]

I pray that this book will prove such a challenge to the reader.

Norman Cliff

[1] C. Rene Padilla, *The New Face of Evangelicalism* (London: Hodder & Stoughton, 1976), 205.
[2] Michael Green, *I Believe in Satan's Downfall* (London: Hodder & Stoughton, 1981), 248.

Abbreviations

CIM   — China Inland Mission
J.B. PHILLIPS — Translation of the Bible by J.B. Phillips
KJV   — King James Version
KMT   — Kuomintang (Guomindang): *a nationalist party founded in China under Sun Yat-sen in 1912*
LBC   — London Bible College
NIV   — New International Version
NKJV   — New King James Version
RAB   — Religious Affairs Bureau
TSPM   — Three Self Patriotic Movement
WCEB   — West China Evangelistic Band (*Lin Gong Duan*)
YMCA   — Young Men's Christian Association

Chinese expressions

dan wei — work unit
lao gai — reform-through-labour camp
pu tong hua — Mandarin Chinese

Chronology
of important political and military events
of modern Chinese history

1644–1911
The Qing dynasty

1898–1900
The Boxer Rebellion

1911
Army revolt marks the beginning of the Republic
Sun Yat-sen (1866–1925) is made first provisional
President of the Republic

1921
Chinese Communist Party is formed

1926–1927
Mao Zedong (1893–1976) organizes the peasants
of Hunan Province

1931
Mukden Incident in which Japan invades Manchuria

1934
The Communists' Long March

1937–1945
Japan attacks and conquers most of China
in the Sino-Japanese War
Second World War

1945
Japan surrenders

1949
The Chinese Communist Party takes over mainland China

1951
The Three-Anti, Five-Anti and
Thought Reform Campaigns
Beginning of the Three Self Patriotic Movement

1953–1956
Collectivization begins

1958–1962
The Great Leap Forward

1966–1976
The Cultural Revolution

1976
Mao Zedong dies

1978
Deng Xiaoping is restored to power

1989
Tiananmen Square massacre

1

袁相忱
ALLEN YUAN

(YUAN XIANGCHEN)

This man is not for turning

> Let us go out to [Jesus], then, beyond the boundaries of the
> camp, proudly bearing His "disgrace." For we have no per-
> manent city here on earth, we are looking for one in the
> world to come (Hebrews 13:13–14, J.B. PHILLIPS).

An eighteen-year-old student had finished his homework in a
Beijing suburb, and was putting his books away. What happened
next he has always found hard to describe.

A revelation of God's love and presence overwhelmed him. He
turned off the kerosene lamp, knelt on the ground and with
uncontrolled sobbing confessed his past sins. He had stolen his
grandmother's purse and the toy sword of a neighbour's child. A
flood of wrongdoings came to his mind as he talked to the
Lord—a dishonest act in a shop, bearing grudges towards his
fellow students and cunningly deceiving his mother.

He poured out all these past actions before God in prayer,
and then with a load lifted from his heart, he lit the lamp again
and found that everything around him seemed to have changed.
The following day he shared this recent experience with his
friends at school. This was to be the beginning of a lifetime of

bold witness for his Master.

Eager to have instruction in the Christian faith, the young convert went to hear Pastor Wang Mingdao at the Christian Tabernacle in Shi Jia Hu Tong in the centre of Beijing.[1] The style of this new building was simplicity itself, perhaps on the austere side. On the white marble foundation stone were engraved the words:

> *He died for our sins.*
> *He rose from the dead.*
> *He ascended to heaven.*
> *He will come again to receive us.*
> *Summer, 1937*

The interior too lacked any religious symbols. At the front in the centre was the pulpit, and in front of that the baptistery. Both externally and internally the church was free from all ecclesiastical trappings. Pastor Wang Mingdao had said in one of his sermons:

> Today the majority of churches have fallen into a very pitiful condition. Many resplendent and magnificent, beautiful and ornate church buildings are like this.
>
> Inside they have fine fittings, comfortable seats, melodious instruments, harmonious choirs, copper crucifixes and snow-white candles. The priest wears a formal black robe, a beautiful sash at his waist, reads from a deluxe edition of the prayer book, and preaches an eloquent sermon.
>
> Today many churches in the world are like this. Only the eyes of God and the eyes of those who understand God's will can see their emptiness.[2]

---

[1] On Wang Mingdao, see his autobiography, *A Stone Made Smooth* [tr. Arthur Reynolds] (Southampton: Mayflower Christian Books, 1981).
[2] Kim-Kwong Chan and Alan Hunter, *Prayers and Thoughts of Chinese Christians* (London: Mowbray, 1991), 33.

Young Yuan listened to such sermons by Wang Mingdao and immediately felt at home in this church building which was crowded with some 700 worshippers. The preaching was powerful, understandable and, most important of all, it answered some of the questions in the mind of this young Christian. Not long afterwards Yuan was baptized by the famous preacher. Twenty years later the two would be standing together against the pressures of a new Communist regime and suffering for it.

At this time the Shandong Revival was bringing renewal to the churches in the nearby province of Shandong, and churches in the neighbouring provinces gladly shared in the blessing that was being experienced. Principal Cui of the YMCA invited Yuan to a meeting to be held in his home where a preacher from Shandong would be speaking. It was at the third meeting in this home attended by Yuan that he had a further deep spiritual experience.

Yuan recalled, "Mr. Cui came up to me, laid his hands on me and prayed for me. I don't know what he prayed about, but I began to weep…I have been a different person since that evening."

In 1934, at the age of twenty, Yuan Xiangchen decided to quit high school and study the Bible. It was not an easy decision to make and it brought him criticism from his family, for he was an only child, and his parents were looking to him for their support in the future.

For four years he studied at a Bible School run by the Oriental Missionary Society, and at the end of this course, which he found most beneficial, he began preaching regularly and "living by faith." It was at this time of living with no fixed salary that he met Miss Liang Huizhen. She was fully in sympathy with his desire to serve the Lord and to look to him for his daily needs. They were married in 1938, and Huizhen was to prove an ideal partner, sharing with Yuan in all the trials and crises of the years which were to follow.

Soon after this he met John Pattee, a missionary of the Church of the Nazarene. In 1940 Pattee asked him to commence work

Allen Yuan sat under the powerful preaching of Wang Mingdao (above) at the Christian Tabernacle in Shi Jia Hu Tong, Beijing

for this mission in nearby Hebei province. The Sino-Japanese War was on, and in spite of the movements of Japanese soldiers, who were on duty in key positions throughout the province, Yuan had regular tent meetings in the villages and was encouraged when many of his fellow countrymen professed faith in Christ.

This was a happy and fruitful period in Yuan's life. At the end of 1941, following the Japanese attack on Pearl Harbor, the United States and Britain declared war on Japan. The Japanese sent all enemy nationals in north China to an internment camp in Weifang. John Pattee went into internment, and for the next three years Yuan continued his evangelistic work in Hebei province. It was not easy as Japanese troops were in occupation. Amid battles and skirmishes between the Japanese and the 8th Route Army, Yuan faithfully continued his work of preaching and witnessing. Various gifts, some financial, from believers provided support for Yuan's wife and three children. Throughout this period they lived frugal and self-denying lives.

It was a relief when the long Sino-Japanese War came to an end in August 1945, but unfortunately that did not mean that peace had come. Fighting continued between the Communist and KMT troops, and the civil war went on for another four years.

Just at this time word came from Beijing that Yuan's mother was critically ill, and so he travelled there with his family in order to be with her. On arrival he found that his mother urgently needed medical treatment, but there were no funds. Yuan had a heavy heart and in his moment of need he slipped into a church, praying earnestly for a double miracle—that his mother would be healed and that she would come to faith. Yuan Xiangchen recalls, "In her sick bed one night my mother had a vision. She saw a man wearing a white gown. The man gave her a yellow powder to eat."

A few hours later Yuan's grandmother arrived at the house with some medicine for his mother. But she refused it and announced that through her unusual dream she had been healed. Not long after this she was baptized, and Yuan's grandmother also came to believe.

For the next three years Yuan preached in a rented building in Fucheng Men Nei Da Jie. During the war it had been used by Orita Kaneo, a Japanese pastor. Yuan's strategy was to commence services in the open air, attract the attention and interest of the people on the street and get them to follow him into the church. He says, "Three times a week we beat a drum to start our meetings, and we distributed tracts and books." Each year he baptized between twenty and fifty new believers.

The work was steadily growing, but the political situation made the future of Christian work quite uncertain. A bitter civil war was being waged throughout China. There was every indication that the Communist forces would gain control of the country. On October 1, 1949 Mao Zedong announced, in Tiananmen Square, the formation of the People's Republic of

China to two million people with the significant sentence, "We have now stood up."

Under the new regime, sixty churches in Beijing, of many denominations, were pressed to join the newly formed Three Self Patriotic Movement and operate under the direction of the government's Religious Affairs Bureau. Religious groups throughout the capital had a crisis on their hands. How should they respond to this situation? Yuan attended a private meeting of a dozen well-known independent preachers to discuss this vital matter. All were unanimous that they could not join the TSPM without compromising their faith.

This was to prove a costly decision. In August 1955 Wang Mingdao, a leader of this dissident group, was arrested after a Sunday evening service, and Yuan's turn came soon afterwards. Fifty-five year old Wang and forty-four year old Yuan were given *life sentences*. Wang was sent to a prison in Taiyuan in Shanxi province, while Yuan was transported to a prison on China's northern border with Russia.

Life in the Heilongjiang prison was far from easy. The weather was bitterly cold, and labouring for nine hours a day in the wheat fields was physically wearying. Although the food was quite inadequate, Yuan kept relatively fit, though he lost a lot of weight. Many of his fellow prisoners could not cope with these harsh conditions and fell ill and died.

In these difficult days Yuan had no Bible to read and no hymn book from which to sing. Nor were there any fellow believers with whom to have fellowship. He formed some common ground with four Catholic priests, who had refused to join the Catholic Patriotic Association, just as he had refused to join the TSPM. They were also bravely labouring in the fields month in and month out with little prospect of ever being free again.

Humanly speaking there was little to live for. Life imprisonment surely meant life imprisonment. For Yuan the future only held the unpleasant prospect of labouring year after year in the rice fields until he died. He recalled to me, "I was far from home and fully expected to die as a martyr on the northern border."

For ten years he wondered if he would ever hear from his family again. Had they forgotten him? Did they think that he had died? Then one day, in the eleventh year of his sentence, a letter reached him. He recognized his wife's handwriting. It gave brief news of herself and their six children. When he went to sleep that night on his hard bed his mind was active, for his memory had been re-awakened. He thought of his large family far away in Beijing. His children were growing up without the guidance of a father. His wife, Liang Huizhen, had to work all day to support them, to feed and clothe them. She had to bring them up single-handed. He might never see them again. Had he not been given a life sentence? If he were released would the children know who he was, and would they accept him as their father? With a heavy heart he could only commit them to his heavenly Father's care.

What was happening to Yuan's family all those long years while he was doing heavy physical work in the far north of China?

At the time when Yuan left Beijing, Liang Huizhen had six children and a mother-in-law to feed, and no employment with which to support them. After her husband's departure as a prisoner she was told that she fell into the category of "anti-revolutionist." She had always enjoyed the love and fellowship of their local church, but now the members had been ordered to avoid all contact with her and her family. Mrs. Yuan found this very hurtful, but she understood that the Christians could not take any risks by disobeying this instruction. From a human standpoint she and her family were doomed to slow starvation. They were penniless, and their stock of food was fast diminishing.

The load which she was now carrying seemed too heavy for her, and she admits that she went through a time of bitterness. "Why do we have to suffer in this way?" she cried out to God one day.

"It is through faithfulness to you that Xiangchen is far away in prison suffering maltreatment." Day after day she argued with God, telling him that she just could not carry such a heavy burden.

But the answer came suddenly. God seemed to be saying to his child, "This thing is from me." She recalls, "These words went deeply into my heart. Immediately I felt strong and able to face the future." She knelt down and prayed, "O God, if this is from you I will no longer argue but obey." After that spiritual struggle and her promise to surrender to the Lord, the burden was gone. Many difficulties and tests were still to come, but she now felt carried along in the arms of her God.

The family then moved into a smaller house to save expenses. Mrs. Yuan had no employment, no weekly income. The Psalmist says, "No good *thing* will he withhold from them that walk uprightly" (Psalm 84:11, KJV). During the difficult months in which Mrs. Yuan had no work, the family's needs were provided in a miraculous way. Just a few examples of this will suffice.

One night Huizhen went to bed without a cent towards the next day's food. At the same time she felt strangely free from anxiety. Ringing in her ears were our Lord's words:

> Take no thought for your life, what ye shall eat, or what ye shall drink; nor yet for your body, what you shall put on... Behold the fowls of the air: for they sow not, neither do they reap, nor gather into barns; yet your heavenly Father feedeth them. Are ye not much better than they?
> (Matthew 6:25-26, KJV)

Early the next morning there was a knock at the door. Mrs. Yuan found an old lady outside. She asked, "Is your husband's name Yuan and yours Liang?" "Yes," said Mrs. Yuan. The stranger went on to say that God had instructed her to find the family and give them help. She had been to the old address, as well as the police station and finally found them. She gave the mother an envelope, in which she found 50 yuan. Mrs. Yuan asked her who she was. She would only say, "God sent me here. Thank him for this." With a heart full of happiness and gratitude Huizhen went to the market and bought food for the family.

On another occasion one of her sons needed equipment for his math lesson at school, costing 16.40 yuan. Huizhen made this a matter of prayer, and soon afterwards she found an envelope under the front door with 25 yuan in it.

Winter was coming, and in Beijing it can be very severe. Her youngest child desperately needed some warm shoes. Again she prayed specifically about this urgent need, and after that she found an envelope in the doorway containing 15 yuan.

In each of these cases and many others Mrs. Yuan wrote letters of thanks, asking the donors to come and visit her. But on each occasion the letters were returned "addressee not known." It seemed that God was teaching her who was truly behind these gifts.

Huizhen knew that she had to find work to support her large family, but she had neither experience nor qualifications, having been a full-time mother for many years. It would have to be a case of accepting whatever opening came her way. Eventually she found a job in a construction company at 24 yuan a month. At first this gentle housewife had to do heavy manual work, but soon she was doing clerical work in the office. Although she knew nothing about accounts and office routine she applied herself to the work she was given, and soon won her boss' trust and approval.

When the Cultural Revolution commenced, and with it the harsh treatment to be meted out to all who were not loyal members of the Communist party, Mrs. Yuan was reminded that she belonged to an "anti-revolutionary" family. This meant that she had to leave the more sheltered work in the construction office and once again do heavy manual work. The night before the changeover she fervently prayed, "O God, I will need your strength."

Mrs. Yuan had to push wheelbarrows loaded with bricks, she had to mix cement with a heavy spade and throw bricks up to the bricklayers. In this harsh environment of back-breaking work there were often moments of welcome assistance by strangers. A workman, seeing this cultured lady struggling to throw up the bricks, came down a ladder and gave her help. Every gesture of humanity made the day's work more manageable.

The construction company moved from one job to the next to various sites in and around Beijing. This meant longer journeys to work. The bitterly cold months of winter arrived, and Mrs. Yuan had to continue doing the same work on the slippery roads. Her hands and feet were numb with the cold, but she was aware of an unseen hand giving her strength and courage to keep going.

The Communist regime affected the lives of Christian families in many subtle ways. When Mrs. Yuan's children applied for higher education the door was closed in their faces because their parents were not party members. When they applied for jobs they were unsuccessful because the "work unit" found out that the applicant's father was a "criminal in jail for life." It was hurtful for the mother of the family to find that her children were suffering from political discrimination in both education and employment. Would it make them bitter and resentful about their parents' firmly held beliefs?

But there were more pressures on Mrs. Yuan to give up her faith and enjoy the privileges which other people had. Corruption was rife and she saw her colleagues at work giving in to bribes, and taking items home which had been purchased for the building work. Pilfering was going on regularly at the work site, and fellow workers noticed that she scrupulously avoided taking anything which was not hers. Her superiors urged her to resort to corruption so that she could have more money for her family's needs. They pressed her to give up her faith, join the Party and be able to avail herself of many of the privileges involved.

Mrs. Yuan was an attractive lady. The men in her company urged her to divorce her husband. "You will never see him again. You might as well re-marry." Men came to her office with propositions, and some visited her at home. To all these pressures the Christian mother gave a firm "No." She states that looking back she recalls that a strange peace came to her as a special gift from God. "I was given a strange calmness amid all these temptations. My enemies wrung no concessions from me. I felt that nothing and no one could harm me because I was in my heavenly Father's arms."

In 1976 the harsh years of the Cultural Revolution came to an end. Christians were no longer subjected to the same degree of unfair discrimination. Mrs. Yuan was asked by her boss to work in the office again, away from the back-breaking work of past years on the building sites. This was a relief for she had experienced sharp pains doing such heavy work. Then the following year she turned sixty, and was given the opportunity to retire. This was something that she welcomed, for it meant a pension and a chance to work in a more leisurely way at home for her family.

She summed up the hard lessons of those difficult years by quoting from Psalm 68:4b–6:

> …rejoice before him. A father of the fatherless, and a judge of the widows, *is* God in his holy habitation. God setteth the solitary in families: he bringeth out those who are bound with chains. (KJV)

But that is to run ahead of our story.

We return now to Yuan Xiangchen in the faraway Heilongjiang prison.

For the prisoners working in the wheat fields there was a break each day at noon. During this welcome respite most of Yuan's fellow prisoners went down to their cells for a smoke. But he walked back and forth in the open air singing two songs that he could remember from his days of freedom. One was based on

Psalm 27 and the other was *The Old Rugged Cross*. The Chinese translation of the chorus of this latter hymn meant a lot to this brave prisoner:

> *So I will lift up my voice and praise the Lord's Cross,*
> *Till before the Lord's throne I see the Father's face,*
> *I will then hear Him say, "Faithful servant—*
> *You can exchange the Cross for the crown of*
> *righteousness."*

This hymn helped him to see beyond his present suffering and his seemingly unending, back-breaking labour to the day when he would see his Master face to face.

Yuan Xiangchen was in one of China's many dreaded *lao gais*, the purpose of which was "reform through labour." The prisoner was to be subjected to all kinds of hardship and isolation with a view to his reviewing the attitudes and convictions of the past, and learning to accept the principles of the new regime in China. Every evening, after long hours of labour in the fields, lectures were given on government policy and on the importance of being good and loyal citizens of the New China.

Reports were regularly submitted to the head of the prison on each individual prisoner. Was he working satisfactorily? Had he changed his attitude and views? For the sake of early release some fell into line with the requirements of their superiors, and gave an impression of acceptance of the new regime's beliefs.

But there was one prisoner who would not budge an inch— Yuan Xiangchen. It was clear to the prison officials that this man had no intention of changing his views. After the evening lectures there was an opportunity for questions and discussion. Yuan had a way of always asking awkward questions.

When he had been in prison for over ten years, one evening he stood up at question time and asked, "What has happened to Liu Shaoqi? There has been no news of him recently. Does this mean that there are disagreements within the Party?" It was a question that the lecturer had no wish to answer. Yuan's hunch that something serious had gone wrong among the Party leaders was quite correct. Liu Shaoqi, former Chief of State, and Deng Xiaoping, Secretary General of the Party, had been denounced by Mao Zedong as "number one traitors who were following the capitalist road." They had been denounced, detained and publicly humiliated.

To the prison officials this was the last straw. Yuan was branded as "an impenetrably thickheaded and downright reactionary." He was placed in a cell four metres by two. His conditions now were immeasurably worse. There was no sunshine or fresh air. Three times a day food was pushed through a hole in the door. To make sure that he did not attempt suicide, all buttons were taken off his clothes and his belt was removed. Guards peeped in at him through the cracks in the door to see how he was behaving. Yuan sat inside this cramped cell cross-legged, where he was supposed to be engaged in self-examination. Instead he was praying to God for strength and peace of mind. As the guards peeped in and saw the prisoner with his eyes shut, perhaps they thought that he was carrying out the self-examination which he had been instructed to do.

This harsh punishment lasted for six months. When Yuan came out of his cramped cell to join the other prisoners his body was stiff and weak, his vision seriously impaired and his clothes crawling with bugs. He was now sixty-two years old. Every step he took caused him acute pain. He longed for a bath and an issue of clean clothes. He realized that even if he had a Bible he might not be able to read it now. But what he could do he did. Morning and evening he closed his eyes and committed himself to God, committed his loved ones, about whom he knew so little and who seemed so far away, to the loving care of his heavenly Father.

The long and crushing Cultural Revolution was beginning to peter out, a revolution in which millions of people had been uprooted from their normal lives and forced to work in the countryside or to languish in China's many prisons. With the continual arrests and detentions the country's prisons and labour camps (*lao gais*) were now taxed to the limit. The inmates were living in cruelly cramped conditions. The prison administration was finding the running of these institutions utterly unmanageable.

Happily, following the death of Mao, Deng Xiaoping became China's new leader, and he began to relax the harsh conditions prevailing throughout the country. Rigid policies were slowly modified and some radically changed. China's citizens, who had been through a traumatic ten years of upheaval and deep suffering, now seemed to vaguely see light at the end of the tunnel. The nation had hit rock bottom and conditions were changing for the better, even though there was still a long way to go before normal and peaceful living could be restored.

And so one day Yuan heard some startling news. Deng had announced that all prisoners who were over sixty years of age and who had been imprisoned for more than twenty years would be released. Their prolonged time in prison had surely rendered them harmless to the Communist programme. Yuan had been sentenced to life imprisonment and had become resigned to spending his life in prison, and even dying there. But as he listened to the two conditions under which prisoners were to be released he realized that he qualified, as did his old colleague Wang Mingdao who had been languishing in prison in Taiyuan, Shanxi.

Yuan could hardly believe this sudden prospect of freedom. But one day, after twenty-one years and eight months of harsh imprisonment, he walked out of his Heilongjiang prison a free man, and travelled south to his home in Beijing. Many thoughts went through his mind as he took the journey back to his loved ones. He was weak in body, his eyesight was poor, and every movement brought pain and discomfort. But God had heard his prayers and his future was in God's hands.

When the preacher arrived at his front door the family saw a

Pastor and Mrs. Yuan outside their humble home and house church in Beijing. Yuan Xiangchen was imprisoned for over twenty-one years in a Heilongjiang prison in north China, before being released in 1977 and reunited with his family.

man who had been through much suffering, thin and weak after all his physical labours and confinement. A joyful family reunion followed. When Yuan had left home twenty-one years earlier there were eight people in his family. Now there were three generations and twenty-four people. There was a lot of catching up to do with children who were now adults, and grandchildren he had never seen.

Yuan had only the torn and stained clothing he had arrived in. Huizhen was now drawing a pension and had some savings, and so they went out and bought some new clothes. Other items came from fellow Christians who were overjoyed to have their leader back again.

Good food served to build up his strength. Love and understanding were shown by his large family. But there was still one more hitch. Upon his return he was not given an identity card, giving him the rights of a Chinese citizen. Yuan was put on probation for a further ten years. He had no freedom to leave his house or to travel.

As was the experience of Paul when under house arrest in Rome, Yuan utilized what limited freedom he had to its maximum advantage. People came to him daily for spiritual advice. He spoke to and prayed with many visitors, and they invariably went away with sound advice as to what steps they should take in their future work. Yuan recalled to me, "I spent much time sharing with them about Jesus, while my wife cooked all through the day to look after these visitors."

Yuan made tape recordings on Christian doctrine and living, and the visitors took the tapes to their homes in Hebei and Henan. Bible study meetings developed into a house fellowship, and from this meeting some of those who had been trained formed house groups in other parts of the capital. Soon this lively house church in western Beijing became one of the best known in the city. I have preached in this home—some eighty people were crowded into a single room, for that is all the space the Yuans have. The lane leading to it is narrow and rough, and twenty yards from the door is the community toilet.

On October 4, 1989 all restrictions on Yuan Xiangchen were lifted. He then had full Chinese citizenship once again, and was able to go wherever he wanted. My first visit to this house church was in 1990, when Yuan had had full citizenship for less than a year. There I met Christian visitors from Taiwan, Hong Kong and from the West. On the wall was a picture of Mr. and Mrs. Yuan sitting opposite Billy and Ruth Graham at a recent banquet held in Beijing. The world-famous evangelist and his wife have visited this humble home on several occasions when passing through Beijing.

In 1996 there was a nationwide swoop on the unregistered church groups. There were arrests and enforced closures, and this fellowship in the west of Beijing did not escape the cleanup. On July 30, 1996, Section Chief Li of the Xichang District, together with two government colleagues, arrived and during a long discussion demanded that Yuan register his meeting place with the Religious Affairs Bureau. The house church which had brought spiritual instruction and help over nearly twenty years was forced to close.

In one of his letters to me Yuan wrote:

> We are experiencing many limitations, but the work is marching on as in the Apostles' time. On August 2, we baptized 252 in Beihai Park. We had rented the children's swimming pool for two hours, costing 400 yuan. Many watched and we just preached to them.
>
> Now our problem is registration, without which we cannot continue our meetings. "The gates of Hell shall not prevail against the church." Please keep praying for China.

2

崔可石
ESTHER CUI

(CUI KOSHI)

The geographer who became an evangelist

> *It seemed 'twere better far*
> *To follow the career I'd choose,*
> *Than let some mighty Power*
> *Turn my course at His high will.*
> —Betty Thornton

The Yangtze River runs through the province of Anhui from the southwest to the northeast. Two thirds of the province is north of this river, and one third south of it. At the time of this story the port city of Anqing was the capital of Anhui province. Eastwards from Anqing and on the south side of the river is Jiuhuashan, where one of China's four sacred Buddhist mountains is situated.

Christian missions to Anhui commenced in 1868, when two intrepid pioneers, James Williamson and James Meadows of the China Inland Mission came to Anqing, living initially on a boat and then renting rooms in the town. Paul, quoting from Isaiah 52:7 says, "How beautiful are the feet of them that preach the gospel of peace, and bring glad tidings of good things!" (Romans 10:15, KJV). These brave workers were assaulted and their home plundered, but they struggled on. Two years later, however, they requested Hudson Taylor transfer them to another centre, saying of the local populace that "everyone stands aloof, and we feel that neither the rulers nor the people are to be trusted."

A decade later William Cooper, newly arrived from Britain, was sent to work in Anqing with the task of making a fresh start and opening up the whole province for Christian witness. Cooper resolved to follow the J.L. Nevius method of "self-reliance from the beginning," with the appointing of Chinese preachers who were to be supported by their own people, free from foreign subsidies (Nevius had successfully used this strategy in Shandong). Slowly but surely the gospel spread through Anhui, and workers from other societies began to arrive. By the time Esther Cui,[1] whose story I am about to tell, was born in 1914 there were several small established churches in Anqing, as well as mission schools.

Anhui has produced some famous people. In the Sung Dynasty (A.D. 970–1127) the family of Zhu Shi, the great expositor of the Chinese classics, came from this province. Then there was Zhu Hongwu, who founded the Ming Dynasty (1364–1644). More recently there was Li Hongzhang (1823–1901), a leading states-man in north China in the late nineteenth century. Although Esther Cui, a daughter of Anhui, never became famous, her sub-sequent work for God in Sichuan province was to be greatly blessed by God.

Esther's birth was a source of bitter disappointment to her maternal grandfather. When her mother was pregnant her grand-father was adamant that the baby, which was due to be born at the Chinese New Year, would be a boy. In his imagination he pictured himself being warmly congratulated by his friends on having a grandson, when they came round at the forthcoming festive season. He thought also of the joy which he would have

---

[1] At that time her surname was spelt "Ts'ui," following the Wade-Giles system of transliteration. Later the Pinyin system was introduced, and her name was spelt "Cui."

in helping to bring up the little boy—helping him to mouth his first words, teaching him to take his first steps and so on.

With this in mind the grandfather bought special food for his expectant daughter to eat to make sure that the hoped-for boy would be strong and healthy. He moved his bed against the wall next to his daughter's room, so that he would be the first to hear the good news. But when he heard that a girl had been born he was angry and bitterly disappointed. He banged on the wooden wall between them, and declared how useless a daughter would be. This was a common attitude in those days, which to some extent still persists in China today. But the newborn baby girl was to grow up to become a most useful person in the service of God.

The earliest influences on the young girl were Christian ones. Although her father, a middle school teacher, made no profession of faith, her mother was a devout Christian, who encouraged her daughter to pray and sing choruses.

St. Agnes School, the primary school to which Esther went for the first stage of her education, was run by missionaries of the American Church Mission. Here she learned the stories of Adam and Eve, of Moses leading the children of Israel out of Egypt, of David and Goliath, of the life of Jesus of Nazareth and of the disciples who followed him. These became the foundation for her spiritual life in later years.

Initially life for the bright and alert young student was happy and secure, but then things took a tragic turn that changed everything. By the time she entered the senior middle school her whole family, parents and siblings, had died one by one and she was now an orphan, left completely on her own. Staying with her grandparents she felt desolate and alone. It was hard to continue applying herself to her studies with the same fervour, for she missed her family keenly. As she walked home from school each day she would remind herself of some verses which she had learned at St. Agnes School about God being the heavenly Father of orphans. She would cling to this thought and found real consolation in it.

Some of the teachers in the middle school took a personal interest in this bright but sad-looking student. Their gestures of love and help made her school days happier and more bearable. The turning point for Esther at this time came when God sent into her life someone who would give her just the help which she was needing as she thought about her future. Dr. Wu Yifang, the first woman principal in China, came to visit the schools in Anqing. When she met Esther, the teenage girl blurted out her ambition to do further study in the Ginling College. But, she confessed, she had no funds for this.

Dr. Wu took an immediate interest in this promising student. She listened to her story, thought for a moment and then said, "I would like to help you to get to Ginling. Take the college's entrance examinations, and if you pass I will see that you can study there and have the necessary funds."

For Esther Cui this was a major breakthrough. She worked hard and passed the exams with high marks. God had sent this kind woman into her life just at the right time, for Dr. Wu obtained a scholarship for Esther that enabled her to complete her college education.

In 1937, Miss Cui graduated in science from the prestigious Ginling College in Nanjing. Then for three years she taught geography in the Fuxiang Middle School. In 1940 her friend Dr. Wu asked her to take up a post as Assistant in the Geography Department at her alma mater, Ginling College. With the heavy bombings of cities by Japanese planes this college had moved from Nanjing to Chengdu in Sichuan, southwest China.

Esther had great ambitions to progress in her chosen field, geography, and to become a researcher and specialist in some branch of this science. She dreamed that she would research the features of the world's rivers and mountains, come to understand the movements of wind and air pressure as regards climate, and in general become an acknowledged authority on some facet of geography. She would go abroad, sit at the feet of famous scientists and deliver academic lectures to eager student audiences.

Step-by-step her career was developing. In 1942 she came to Beibei, thirty miles north of Chongqing, to work in the government's Geographical Institute as a research assistant. Little did she realize that Beibei would be her home base for the remainder of her life. Although she was not aware of it God was slowly leading her forward. He had other plans for her.

Beibei had recently been built as a model town by the Chinese government, and had been placed in a strategic position at a point north of Chongqing, which was then the capital of Sichuan. Its streets were paved and its houses made of well-constructed brick and stone. It soon had six middle schools, two teacher training colleges, the Science Institute of West China, the College of Accountancy and a university. Thus it was to be a strong co-educational centre. Beibei was to prove to be a success story for the Sichuan provincial government.

The Chinese have a saying that "a journey of a thousand miles begins with a single step." For Esther Cui that first single step resulted from something that happened in 1944, changing her life and her ambitions for the future.

Archdeacon Vyvyan Donnithorne, a former missionary of the Church Missionary Society, had recently formed the West China Evangelistic Band (WCEB, in Chinese *Lin Gong Duan*). This small and fervent society described itself as a "community of Christians who are pledged to live and work together in one house as one family in Jesus Christ, to devote themselves to the work of spreading the gospel." Its founder, Vyvyan Donnithorne, stated in the first newsletter that they looked to the Christian ashrams in India as their role model. He came to Beibei with a team of keen young Chinese students, eager to share the gospel with their fellow countrymen. These young men had come with thousands of other students to southwest China, part of one of the greatest treks in human history. Fleeing the Japanese occupation on the east coast, they had travelled by anything which moved—bicycles, wheelbarrows, trucks and trains—to Sichuan to continue their studies, already so badly disrupted by the war.

In their new surroundings they had attended Christian meetings, where they had made firm commitments to Jesus Christ. Through regular Bible studies and warm fellowship with older Christians, these new disciples had been built up in their new-found faith. Eager to share this with others, they had joined the West China Evangelistic Band as voluntary workers, taking meetings in the main centres in Sichuan.

Coming to Beibei, the evangelistic team found that they had "struck gold." This strategic town had had no missionary influence. The WCEB purchased some land, and on it built a compound, in which was a church with rooms used by the Donnithornes, and another building in which was a dining room, classroom and bedrooms for the Band's workers and students. The structure was in harmony with the Band's desire to live a communal life.

In the centre of Beibei the evangelistic team erected a spacious tent, seating 300 people, and advertised special meetings. The publicity was successful for the tent was filled four times a day for several weeks.

Twenty-five year old Esther was told about the meetings and began to attend. What she heard reminded her of her Christian upbringing many years earlier in Anhui province. Esther had stopped attending church or studying the Christian faith since her college days.

Before the meetings were over Esther Cui's interest in the Christian life had been aroused. She had a long talk with Miss Liao Enzhong, one of the Band's workers, and made a firm commitment to be a disciple of Jesus Christ. She joined the small group of believers and shared in its meetings of prayer and fellowship. Gladys Donnithorne, the leader's wife, took a special interest in the young research assistant who had begun attending the believers' meetings, and encouraged her to take part in the church's activities.

Within a few months Esther left her work in the laboratory, and with it her long-held ambitions. She went to nearby Chongqing to study the Bible at the Spiritual Light Seminary of Pastor Jia Yuming. Jia was known throughout China as one of the country's finest expositors. The seminary had a choice location. It was situated amid thick pine woods at the top of one of the steep hills that line the south bank of the Yangtze River at Chongqing. The seminary property on this hill consisted of a chapel, a school hall, some classrooms and the residences for faculty and students.

Looking back to the three years spent at the seminary, Esther feels that it was here that she received an excellent grounding in biblical studies and theology, which stood her in good stead for the difficult years which were to lie ahead, as well as for the many years as a pastor's wife. In the quietness and breathless beauty of these grounds she learned to communicate with her Master and listen to his voice. While at the Spiritual Light Seminary she had a great deal of contact with its beloved principal, Pastor Jia, who inspired her to live a life of total dedication. In those days before such facilities as photocopying Jia often asked Esther to copy out some of his spiritual writings, and in the process of carrying out this task she absorbed much of his devotional thought.

Gladys Donnithorne continued to maintain a close interest in this keen and well-educated young lady. Esther had intellectual qualities as evidenced by her earlier university studies and her recent studies at the Spiritual Light Seminary. She also had the spiritual qualities of humility, gentleness and insight. The Sino-Japanese War was now over, and the church in Sichuan would need dedicated indigenous workers such as Esther Cui. In the WCEB Newsletter of August 1947 Archdeacon Donnithorne says of her, "She is a young woman of great mental ability, and is greatly appreciated as an evangelist to educated people." But she was not only an evangelist, she was also described as "the Band's worker among children."

And so Mrs. Donnithorne, who had become her spiritual mother, found the funds for Esther to study overseas. It was a bold step for young Esther, after completing her studies in Chongqing, to leave her native land to do further theological studies in far away Britain, involving as it did working in a foreign language.

In the summer of 1947 Esther Cui bade farewell to her colleagues in the West China Evangelistic Band. She flew from Chongqing to Shanghai, and went by boat to Britain via the United States. The London Bible College (LBC), with its fine building on Marylebone Road in the centre of London, had only been running a few years when Esther Cui arrived in the capital. Dr. Ernest Kevan, the Principal, gave her a warm welcome. Although there were students at the college from many countries, Esther was his first pupil from mainland China. Her first challenge was English, but soon she was able to understand what the lecturers were saying, and was taking a full part in the life of the college.

Esther Cui's heart and thoughts were with the Band in Beibei. The Newsletter of October 1947 said, "We have been delighted to hear from Esther, and also to hear from English friends how well she has been received at home. She represents the very first fruits of our work in Beibei, as she got in touch with the Band at the first meeting held there."

She made many friends at the London Bible College. Her closest friends were Scandinavian, and they invited her in the college holidays to visit their homes on the Continent. She addressed church gatherings and was overwhelmed by the welcome that she received from these warm-hearted people.

Esther never forgot her visit to the great Keswick Convention in the Lake District of England. She recalls being called upon to speak at the missionary meeting and addressing 5,000 people. Trembling with nervousness, she spoke to the large audience about her clear call to return to China to work among her own people. She was convinced, she said in her brief address, that whatever the political situation might be, God needed her in the land of her birth.

During the Sino-Japanese War and in the years following, a bitter civil war had been raging across Esther's beloved motherland. Communist forces were clearly getting the upper hand, and if they came to power there would be some radical changes in the life and witness of the churches. Undoubtedly things would get more difficult for Christian believers. Esther's English friends pleaded with her to work in Britain, but her thoughts were unquestionably with her own people. Furthermore, the funds that Gladys Donnithorne had given her were running out, and there was the fear of being stuck in Britain when the new regime in China took control.

After a happy year at LBC Esther made plans at the end of 1948 to return to China, and to her circle of Christian friends in Beibei. In October 1948 she was given an enthusiastic send-off at a meeting in Central Hall, Westminster; she sailed for home on October 22.

In China the Communists were continuing to slowly gain control, having advanced through much of the country. In many ways the local people looked forward to a Communist takeover. Inflation was rampant, with money halving in value overnight until paper money was no longer used and people reverted to the age-old custom of using silver dollars or barter trade. On October 1, 1949, less than a year after Esther Cui's return, Mao Zedong stood up in Tiananmen Square in Beijing, and dramatically announced to two million people, "We have now stood up." By this he meant that there would be no more exploitation by or subservience to other nations. China was now to be its own master.

But this "standing up" also included an end to the leadership of Western missionaries in the life of the churches. There was a saying at that time in some circles with regard to those who converted to the Christian faith, "One more Christian, one less Chinese." There was more than a grain of truth in this bitter criticism.

Esther Cui, glad to be back among her own people, began preaching regularly in the Beibei Gospel Church, as the steadily growing fellowship there was now called. She particularly enjoyed her work among the children, to whom she taught choruses and Scripture texts. But her work was not confined to children. Gladys Donnithorne wrote of her in the Newsletter: "Esther and others are out on a country trip. There are so many calls to go to country places, and Esther is the strongest woman worker. I am thankful to say that she feels a real call to preach among the country folk."

The WCEB was now at its peak in membership. There were nineteen Chinese workers, David Day (a newly arrived worker from England), as well as Vyvyan and Gladys Donnithorne. These high figures were soon to drop drastically on account of imminent political events, though the individual workers were to remain true to their faith amid difficult circumstances.

Under the new rulers, changes were taking place all over the country. Esther, however, continued to preach the gospel, leaving politics to the politicians. There was always the hope that freedom to worship and preach would continue. But the atmosphere was slowly changing.

Archdeacon Donnithorne wrote in the Newsletter of November 1951:

> By the end of last year [1950] it was becoming apparent that all missionaries would have to leave the country... In February [1951] I most reluctantly applied for an exit permit, and finally I got permission to leave in July. I had rather an unusual send-off. The church turned out in great force, and we walked in a procession from the compound to the bus station, where I was greeted by more friends. Police and a group of students yelled and hissed at me.

One of the few communications from Esther Cui to the Donnithornes after their departure gives an insight into life under the new Communist rulers:

> Thank you for your prayers. All of us have been kept in safety and "hidden under his wings" in all sorts of difficult circumstances. We have passed through them in peace and safety. Every evening the people in our section of the town meet for indoctrination classes in the Waiting Room of the Clinic.

Vyvyan and Gladys Donnithorne arrived at Tilbury Docks on September 22, 1951. During their furlough they refused to consider settling in Britain. With the door to mainland China closed they found a sphere of service in Hong Kong. At this time thousands of Chinese were pouring over the border into the British colony, to be given accommodation in the Resettlement Camps. It was among these refugees that the Donnithornes found a fruitful sphere of work.

To their new address in Hong Kong came small instalments of news from Beibei—some coded letters from Chinese Christians, some verbally delivered from those who had escaped to the colony. And the news they received was far from rosy.

Back in Beibei Esther Cui had been arrested on March 15, 1952. What had she done to deserve imprisonment? She had returned to China just before "Liberation," and therefore must have been working with Western imperialists.

The Band Newsletter of July 1953 gives more news about the Christians in Beibei:

> Ruth has been able to get out of China, and is now in the colony. Grace and E. [Esther] are "like Paul when he wrote Colossians" [in prison], and now we have learned that Mr. M. [Ma Nianjiao] is living under the same conditions, so the little church at Beibei has been without its leaders for over

a year now... No fault has been found in them, but they are still detained. Cottage meetings are held in several homes, and new believers are being added to the church. So the work of God is still going on.

For this gentle and sensitive lady, Esther Cui, life had taken a rough turn. Prison was no place for a woman of such integrity. It was not long before Esther Cui was identified as someone quite different from the other female prisoners in her group. She could read and write, she cared about hygiene, her face was a picture of composure and she had a bearing that put her in a different class to those around her.

Like Joseph in the Bible who was also falsely charged, she was soon given tasks of responsibility. Esther was put in charge of a "ban-all-smoking" programme. It was her task to keep a register of all prisoners, and a record of which women prisoners continued to smoke. She was authorized to search fellow prisoners and their belongings to see if they had cigarettes. This was an unenviable task, but her gentleness and tact won the day. She was frequently asked, "Why is it that you are so different from us?" But in her reply she was not allowed to make any reference to her Christian faith. She could only vaguely reply that perhaps her upbringing had been different.

In Hong Kong and in Britain Christians were praying for Esther, and were anxious for news of her. Only the briefest message was conveyed in the Newsletter of May 1954: "Thank God that we have heard that Esther is still strong in the faith, and we believe that God will continue to use her life and testimony."

A year later the Newsletter of April/June 1955 gives another small item of news. Regular political indoctrination classes were being held in Esther's prison, and the following comment was added: "She has not returned yet, as she still has not completed her time in bonds." The report went on to say that she had work to do which kept her occupied.

Falsely accused of working for Western imperialists, Esther Cui spent over four years in prison (1952–1956) under Mao Zedong's regime

After another long gap the Newsletter of September/December 1956 merely states: "No news is allowed to come through, so we are left without news of our beloved Esther."

Finally the good news of Esther Cui's release reached Hong Kong, and the Newsletter of January/March 1957 announced: "Most of you have already heard of Esther's release and of her return home. You have been praising God with us for this wonderful answer to prayer."

The four-and-a-half years that Esther spent in prison on false charges could not have been easy. Looking back on this period, she emphasized to me that at no time did she have to do heavy labour, nor was she treated harshly. Her thoughts were often directed to the group of believers to which she belonged. She knew that they would be praying regularly for her. The one link that she had with them was that a young man, Peter Yeh, sent her regular parcels of food during her imprisonment. Peter had been a leading layman in the Beibei church from its earliest days. She was touched by this regular supply of much-needed food.

In the autumn of 1956 Esther Cui was released from prison and happily returned to teaching. There was now a new depth to her ministry. In the long months behind high walls she had learned to trust God in a deeper way than ever before. She was given a warm welcome by her fellow Christians in Beibei.

Esther had always intended to serve God as a single woman. She believed that this freedom from marital responsibilities would enable her to work for God more effectively. But the tender attention of Peter Yeh, the man who had given her practical help during her imprisonment, made her reconsider her strongly held views. Peter was the eldest son in his family and was one of the earliest members of the Band. He had come to Beibei as a civil servant and been converted in his early twenties through the witness of the Band. When he decided to be a full-time Christian worker he had faced criticism and opposition from his father who was not a Christian. He had pressed his son to enter a more lucrative form of employment. In spite of this pressure Peter had gone to the Spiritual Light Seminary and studied there.

An insight into Peter's spiritual motivation is given in the WCEB Newsletter of June 1946 at the time of his graduation from the seminary: "Peter has now returned to us. With his red-hot zeal, his deep love for the Lord Jesus, his abounding high spirits and radiant cheerfulness he is a valuable acquisition to our Team."

Esther was nearly forty and Peter thirty-two. Their cultural backgrounds were quite different. But they had a common love for the Lord, and a shared desire to serve the church in Beibei. So, soon after her release, she married Peter. Together they have served Christ more effectively than they would have done separately.

During the 1950s disquieting news was coming in from all over the country. Communist forces had occupied many church buildings and disrupted normal church life. In all the main cities of China heart-rending "denunciation meetings" were being organized. Before large crowds, respected church leaders were verbally attacking some of the great missionaries of the past, as well as missionaries then living in the West, and most serious of all, missionaries still living in the country. They were all being lumped together as "spies" and "agents of cultural aggression." Chinese bishops made allegations against fellow bishops, and church leaders against their colleagues. Many of those attacked were sent to prison in distant provinces.

After her release from prison Esther was able to teach again for two years. Then in 1958 came a period of restriction, which was to last twenty years. Christian pastors and workers in the area were rounded up and forced to work in a government-owned glove factory. At least this time Peter was with her to share in the restrictions and trials of this period. Together they shared the monotony and deprivations of these years.

They were a motley team of factory workers, for the group included Buddhist monks, Catholic priests and Protestant pastors and workers. Together they worked at making gloves. Esther had no Bible to read. She could only repeat to herself passages with which she was familiar. Nor were there any religious services. But the authorities could not stop the workers praying privately, and this is what both Esther and Peter did.

On the whole the Protestant workers worked together amicably in the production process. But one of their number was the clerk of works, charged with the task of overseeing his colleagues, and paying them at an agreed-upon rate. But when it came to pay day he often withheld part of their remuneration, giving flimsy reasons for doing so and pocketing the difference. He also made false reports about Peter and Esther and other Christian workers. This was one of the trials of doing the compulsory factory work.

The couple must have often wondered what had happened to their church of some 200 members in Beibei. Unbeknownst to them, in 1966 it was forced to close and the small building was taken over for use as a factory. A Mrs. Lo, who lived next door to the church, invited the nucleus of members to meet in her home. This faithful group of believers kept alive a Christian witness in Beibei during these difficult years.

By August 1966, the Cultural Revolution was in full swing. Red Guards went on the rampage attacking the "four olds"— old ideas, old culture, old customs and old habits. These student radicals went systematically down the streets of the big cities stripping the churches, temples and mosques of ornaments and furnishings. Bibles and hymn books were burned, and religious personnel were forbidden to engage in any religious activities. Many were subjected to abuse and ill treatment.

The Christian church went underground. All over China Christians were meeting secretly. The Beibei fellowship was one of hundreds of such groups. Christ had promised, "For where two or three are gathered together in My name, I am there in the midst of them" (Matthew 18:20, NKJV). And so the Beibei fellowship, without the leadership of Peter and Esther, was part of a nationwide phenomenon of faithful believers keeping the light of faith alive in private meetings in people's homes.

For Peter and Esther, an indomitable couple, month after month, year after year went by doing their routine work in the glove factory. But in 1979 events took a favourable turn. A relative of Esther's by marriage put her name forward to teach English to cadres in the Sichuan Instrument Factory. This was an opportunity not to be missed and an opening to be welcomed. She refreshed her knowledge of English, now rather rusty, and made preparations for the lessons that she would be giving. She proved to be a good teacher, and was soon giving courses in advanced English.

After she had been teaching for a year, Peter and Esther found themselves free to come and go as they pleased, after twenty-two years of restrictions. Esther continued teaching English at the Sichuan Instrument Factory, and this became their source of financial support. This change also meant that they could make contact once again with the Beibei fellowship. Every Sunday they went there to lead the services.

By 1985 the church had made considerable progress and the political situation was becoming more relaxed. The government began the process of returning church buildings to the Christians, bearing the cost of repairs and refurbishment. Initially one church building a week in China was returned for worship, though ten years later the ratio was to become three churches every two days. Deng Xiaoping had ushered in an era of greater religious freedom. Pastors who had languished in prisons and on farms in distant provinces doing enforced labour were released to return to their pastorates and discover that their membership rolls had doubled and tripled.

The small Beibei church building erected in 1944 had been occupied and used as a nail factory. When the Christians, taking advantage of Deng's new reforms, asked for their church to be returned, the factory manager eventually replied that they could not find alternative accommodation. The government instructed him to pay the church full compensation. In 1985 the funds were duly received and a new site for a church purchased. It was a happy day when after all the years of trial and tribulation the members had a ceremony, dedicating the new plot of ground to the service of God. The exciting process of construction began immediately and on July 6, 1986 the Beibei Christian Church was completed.

Peter and Esther continued to travel between the Sichuan Instrument Factory and the church. In every way things were looking up. Congregations were increasing, and the Christians were free once again to meet for fellowship.

In March 1988, Peter Yeh was ordained by the Christian Council as a minister of the gospel. The council leaders also wanted to ordain Esther, but she firmly declined. "I am an ex-jailbird," she declared, "and so I am not fit to be an ordained pastor." On this point she was adamant. The church leaders agreed that Peter, with his problem of lameness, would not be expected to attend committee meetings. In retrospect, the couple feel that Peter's exemption from travelling to meetings and Esther's refusal of ordination have worked out for the best, for they have been able to give more time to their local church.

When I first visited Beibei in 1990 Peter and Esther were still working at the Sichuan Instrument Factory in North Hot Springs, and travelling each Sunday to the church to take services. But a few months after my visit they moved to the church premises. Esther was released from teaching at the factory, though the manager was reluctant to lose her services. But now at last they were free to give the church their full-time service.

On my second visit in 1994 extra rooms had been built along-side the church. On the ground floor of this new wing was a large kitchen, from which 700 people were served hot porridge every Sunday at noon. Above it was a row of residential rooms—the first two for Pastor and Mrs. Yeh, then a guest room, and beyond

*Pastor Peter Yeh and Esther Cui standing in front of the enlarged
Beibei Christian Church, Sichuan province, China*

it rooms for church workers. It was my privilege to stay in the guest room, and to have the opportunity to speak each day to their team of workers. Just before that trip I had broken my ankle, and each morning Ms. Chen Shifeng, a retired doctor in traditional Chinese medicine, rubbed ointment on my swollen foot. I learned that one of the features of this church was that members in their retirement were applying their skills for the benefit of the membership.

The building programme of the Beibei church has been remarkable. In 1996 further enlargement took place, and an upper chapel was built so that on a Sunday there are now two auditoriums for the worshippers. A loud speaker system ensures that those in the lower chapel can hear the service. The church has become a centre of love and service, and new families are being attracted to the warm fellowship inside its walls. The officials in the Religious Affairs Bureau (RAB) have long learned to trust Esther Cui. She is gentle and transparently honest in all her dealings with them, and the RAB has in response agreed to the church's requests from time to time to engage in further building plans. Making use of the enlarged premises, which include rooms for visitors, there are regular conferences to which Christians from other parts of the province come. At these gatherings an average of 200 are baptized each year, and join the Beibei church.

Chinese often have their name changed during their childhood. The pronunciation of Esther Cui's name remained unchanged, but the characters were altered. Her original name was "Shi," and the character conveyed the number ten. This was the perfect number, for her father, who did not share his father-in-law's views about baby girls, wanted his child to be a perfect daughter. The same character also meant "the cross," because the symbol of the cross was similar to the number ten.

The girls living near Esther were envious, because her name

could be written with just two strokes of a pen, while they had names which needed many strokes and were more difficult to remember. So her father changed the character for "Shi" to mean "Rock." Her name was still pronounced the same, but now had a different meaning. It was the same character used in the Chinese Bible to record Christ's words to Peter when he said, "On this *rock* I will build My church" (Matthew 16:18, NKJV).

Esther likes to think that both characters for "Shi," though not intended by her father, speak of the two landmarks in her life— her conversion at the *cross* and her service as a *rock* in the building of the church.

⎯⎯▲▲⎯⎯

Esther wrote to me in one of her frequent letters, "The Lord has done great things for this church." And then she quoted from the Book of Acts, "The Lord added to the church daily such as should be saved" (Acts 2:47, KJV). And so the work quietly goes on. Looking back over her long and eventful life, fraught with so many years of suffering, she can truly say with John Newton:

> 'Twas grace that taught my heart to fear,
>   And grace my fears relieved.
> How precious did that grace appear
>   The hour I first believed.
>
> Through many dangers, toils and snares,
>   I have already come.
> 'Tis grace has brought me safe thus far
>   And grace will lead me home.

3

倪柝聲
WATCHMAN NEE

(NI TUOSHENG) 1903–1972

His sermons still challenge Western Christians today

> I am at a loss to convey to you the blessedness of this discovery, that the Holy Spirit dwelling within my heart is a Person. …I am only an earthen vessel, but in that earthen vessel I carry a treasure of unspeakable worth, even the Lord of glory.
> —Watchman Nee[1]

The Fujianese have been called the Anglo-Saxons of China. They are rugged individualists, self-reliant and hard working. We shall see that this was true of Watchman Nee who was born and brought up in this province.

His was a happy home and he was part of a large family. His parents, Ni Wengxui and Lin Heping, were married in 1899. The man around whom this story centres was born in 1903. He was Heping's third child, but more significantly the first son. Eventually there were nine children.

As the first two children were daughters his mother feared that she would follow in the experience of her sister-in-law, who had borne six daughters. So she prayed daily for a son and like Hannah

---

[1] Watchman Nee, *The Normal Christian Life* (3d ed.; London: Victory Press, 1961), 99.

of old told the Lord, "If I bear a son I will present him to you."
When Nee was born she was determined to keep her promise.

It was certainly a happy childhood. Heping, in spite of the size
of her young family and the many duties involved in bringing
them up, taught each of her children the stories of the Bible and
the hymns of the church from an early age. But Wengxui and
Heping did not want to do this at the expense of their children
being unfamiliar with their own Chinese culture. There was a
complaint in some circles in China that when a person became a
Christian it was a case of "one more Christian, one less Chinese."
Nee's mother made sure that her children also had a good grounding in the rich heritage of their own land. Every week a scholar
came to the home and taught them the Confucian classics.

Watchman Nee's nephew, Stephen Chan, wrote in later years
about his uncle's upbringing:

> My grandfather [Nee's father] invited a classical scholar to
> teach his children. He divided them into two classes. My
> mother, Uncle Nee and an aunt in one class, and the rest of
> the brothers and sisters in another. The text was *The Four
> Books* and the *Five Classics of Confucius*—*The Book of
> Odes* etc. My uncle had a high IQ. Although my mother and
> aunt were older, yet they could not compare with him when
> it came to learning. Most important in the curriculum was
> the writing of essays with a first, second or third place in a
> Hanlin academy exams as the standard sought. My uncle
> usually got a first.[2]

At the age of thirteen, Nee started his studies at the Anglican
Middle School in Fuzhou. This was part of a complex of schools
known as Trinity College. At home he had always spoken in the
Fujian dialect, but now he had to speak the official *pu tong hua*

---

2 Stephen Chan, *My Uncle, Nee Tuosheng* (Translated from the Chinese, 1968), 4.

(official Mandarin). He was a good student and was almost invariably top of the class. Strangely, in view of his future fame as a biblical expositor, the one subject in which he did not do well was religious knowledge. He was antagonistic to the study of the Bible. The prevailing anti-foreign feeling made him harbour hostility to a "Western religion."

But on April 29, 1920 Watchman Nee's life was forever changed, and with it his negative attitude to "Western religion." Miss Dora Yu (Yu Cidu), a preacher from Shanghai, was having special meetings at the local Methodist church. Nee was invited to the services and later recalled:

> I broke down in tears and confessed my sins, and asked the
> Lord to forgive me. I accepted him, and because of his great
> love promised that I would serve him all my life.

Among the things which the young Christian had to do now was to go to his school Principal and confess that he had cheated in his Scripture exams. Before going into the examination room he had written some possible answers on the palm of his hand.

From the very beginning Nee was intense and very zealous about his new-found faith. Looking around his school where many of the pupils professed to be Christians, he felt that though these students attended chapel and joined in the religious activities at this Anglican college, their faith was formal, outward and insincere, and he suspected that many of them attended the Christian meetings with ulterior motives. A local independent lady missionary, Margaret Barber, with whom he discussed these matters, encouraged him to reject the liturgy and formality of Anglican worship. She herself had originally been a missionary of the (Anglican) Church Missionary Society, but had resigned and now worked as an independent missionary in unstructured gatherings, free from fixed prayers and procedures.

Nearly a year after his conversion, on Easter Sunday, March

28, 1921, Ni Tuosheng was baptized as a believer together with his mother and his brother, Ni Huaizu, although he had previously been baptized as an infant. The informal service took place in the river Min and the candidates were baptized by an independent preacher. As he walked into the water for baptism, Nee's inward prayer was:

> Lord, I leave my world behind. Your Cross separates me from it for ever. I am entering into a new world. I stand where you have placed me in Christ.[3]

In later years when he was expounding Romans 6:1-11 (in an address which was published in the book entitled *The Normal Christian Life*) Nee said:

> The real meaning behind baptism is that at the Cross we were 'baptized' into the historic death of Christ, so that His death became ours.... It is to this historic 'baptism'...that we assent when we go down into the water. Our public testimony in baptism today is our admission that the death of Christ two thousand years ago was a mighty all-inclusive death, mighty enough and all-inclusive to carry away in it and bring to an end everything in us that is not of God.[4]

Nee looked for a spiritual home among the churches in Fuzhou and he became critical of the formalism and nominalism which he felt existed. He had many difficult questions to ask about these denominational churches. Why, he asked, did Christians attend the Lord's supper and then go and play a game of mahjong? Why was this supper only celebrated monthly or in some churches only quarterly? He shared these problems with

3 Angus I. Kinnear, *Against the Tide* (Fort Washington, Pennsylvania: Christian Literature Crusade, 1973), 55.
4 *Normal Christian Life*, 66.

Margaret Barber, who shared his concerns. They agreed that he should seek out a group of Christians who really "meant business" with the Lord.

Just at this time he met a young naval officer, Wang Zai (later to be known as Dr. Leland Wang), who had recently resigned his commission in the Chinese navy and had settled in his native town of Fuzhou. Dr. and Mrs. Wang, his brother Wilson Wang (Wang Xi) and Watchman Nee formed a fellowship, meeting regularly in Leland's home. It was a significant step, for from this group grew a new movement in China known as the Little Flock, which was to have assemblies all over China.

This unstructured meeting, with its weekly gatherings for Bible study, prayer and the regular observance of the Lord's supper was precisely what Nee had been looking for. It was informal, free from ecclesiastical traditions and brought to each participant a real sense of the Lord's presence.

After the first occasion when these four had a "Breaking of Bread" service together Nee was overwhelmed with joy and satisfaction. He later said:

> I will never forget it. Never have I felt heaven so close to me as on that evening. I now understand the real meaning of breaking bread in remembrance of the Lord.

These young people were eager to share their faith with others in the town. From their times of study and prayer they went out into the streets of Fuzhou to preach and witness. They did something which became popular half a century later, in that they wore "gospel T-shirts," which had evangelistic texts on them. They beat drums to attract people's attention and sang simple choruses. By this means others joined the small fellowship. To publicize their meetings and their beliefs, Nee edited a small magazine *Revival* (Fuxin Bao).

Unfortunately the honeymoon did not last long. Leland Wang

and Watchman Nee, both strong personalities and of very decided views, differed on several matters. The main issue that divided them was that Wang believed that a pastor should be invited to their meetings, ordain them and they should then be financially supported by their fellow Christians. Nee differed radically. He stood for what he later called "the purity of the testimony," which was that Christian workers did not need ordination and should do their work of preaching, living by faith without regular support.

For Nee it was a painful experience one day in 1923, barely a year since the fellowship had been formed, to be asked to discontinue attending on the grounds that he was too contentious and disturbed the harmony of the meetings. In that brief period, however, he had discovered what he really believed in: a Christian meeting based on New Testament simplicity, free from what he regarded as cramping traditions.

Just after the painful experience of being forced to leave the small group of Christians in Fuzhou, Nee wrote a hymn expressing his sense of rightness in the stand which he had taken:

> *If I'd depart from the right course*
> *I'd have comfort at once,*
> *But I remember my Lord Jesus,*
> *His suffering and loyalty.*
> *Ignoring men's scowlings and spite,*
> *I desire the Lord's smiles.*
> *The crowds enjoy all outward show,*
> *But I long for His best.*[5]

The young preacher continued to have fellowship with other Christians who shared his dissenting views. He was invited to preach in Xiamen, Gulangyu, Zhangzhou and Tong-an. He was fluent and zealous, but his listeners realized that he was pursuing

[5] James Chen, "Meet Brother Nee" (1972), 20–22.

a line that conflicted with the procedures of the established mission churches. From time to time Margaret Barber listened patiently to the unburdening of his problem of spiritual loneliness, and prayed with him. Now that he had broken with Leland Wang's group he began to wonder where he could find another congenial spiritual home. He read and studied the Bible systematically and loved preaching, but in a sense he was a rebel without a cause.

———

At this time in the mid-1920s Nee went out regularly with a group of young preachers to bring the gospel to villages which had not heard the good news. In a sermon which he later preached under the title "There is a God"[6] he recalled a remarkable incident, the truth of which six of the men who had accompanied him and were still alive could corroborate.

The young men entered the village of Wuyue Hua to preach. The villagers would not pay any attention to what they said as they were busy preparing for the annual festival procession in honour of the god Da Wang, who for over two hundred years, the people asserted, had kept rain away during the festivities.

One of Nee's colleagues made a challenge by asserting that this year Jesus would bring rain during the festival. The villagers then promised that they would listen to the young men's preaching and read their booklets if rain came on January 11, the day of the Da Wang festival procession. The seven workers then prayed together for rain on that day in order to prove that Christianity was true.

On the morning of January 11 heavy rain came down until the streets were over three feet deep in water. The man who was carrying the idol Da Wang in the procession fell in the rising water. As he fell the idol also crashed to the ground and was badly damaged. As the rain became heavier the procession had to stop.

The villagers then asserted that the procession should actually

6 Sermon can be found in *Full of Grace and Truth* (New York: Christian Fellowship Publishers, 1980), 1:13–20.

have been on the evening of January 14. The sky was clear for the next three days and again, on the evening of the fourteenth, there was a heavy downpour.

Nee recounts in his published sermon that this incident opened the way for the villagers to listen to the seven young Christian preachers attentively, and that many came to believe.

It was in 1928 that Nee found his life's work. He left his native Fujian and settled in the large metropolitan port of Shanghai, which he saw as a strategic centre for Christian witness. He rented a property on Hardoon Road that seated a hundred people. Convinced of the rightness of forming an autonomous and unstructured assembly, where the Lord's supper was observed every Sunday, he invited Christians in the city to join his fellowship. He wrote, "Those who really want to live entirely in accordance with the Lord's truth will know real freedom in our midst." The preconditions for joining his church were the severing of all links with denominational churches, baptism by immersion and willingness to observe the Lord's supper weekly.

At this time the young preacher wrote a poem in Chinese (similar to the well-known thirteenth-century prayer of Francis of Assisi) which expressed his desire to be of service to God and man. A part of it is as follows:

> *Let me love, but not be thanked,*
> *Let me serve, but not be recompensed.*
> *Let me spend my strength, but not be noted.*
> *Let me suffer much, but not be seen.*
> *Let me pour my wine without drinking.*
> *Let me break my bread without keeping.*[7]

---

7 Chen, "Meet Brother Nee," 100.

Nee began his meetings with some two dozen supporters. In 1932, four years later, he claimed that twenty fellowships had been formed and over 4,000 people had been saved and revived. Slowly but surely new assemblies sprang up in many parts of China. Also some churches of the China Inland Mission as well as other groups went over *en bloc* to what came to be called the Little Flock. Members of these satellite assemblies travelled to Shanghai and Hangzhou to listen to their leader give addresses on the nature of the church and on the believer's spiritual life.

On October 19, 1934, at the conclusion of a ten-day conference which he had led in Hangzhou, Nee married Charity (Zhang Pinhui), an M.A. graduate of Yanjing University in Beijing.

At this stage it is important to trace the stages in the development of this courtship. Twelve years before the marriage Nee fell in love with Charity. He was 19 years old, and she was 18. There was much to commend this prospective relationship. His father, Ni Wengxiu, and Charity's father, Zhang Zhenguan, had played together as children and maintained their friendship through the years. They were in fact distantly related. Charity's father was later to become a pastor in Tianjin.

But there was a problem. Charity had made no profession of faith. In fact she sometimes ridiculed Nee's commitment to Christ, and when he tried to persuade her to believe she laughed at him. Zealous in his new-found faith, Nee had to admit to himself that Charity was worldly and superficial in her lifestyle.

But he was head-over-heels in love with her, and struggled inwardly over her lack of commitment to Christ. When he prayed he pleaded with God to lead Charity into faith. One day when he was preparing a sermon he came across a verse in the Psalms which said, "Whom have I in heaven *but thee*? and *there is* none upon earth *that* I desire beside thee" (Psalm 73:25, KJV).

He knelt down and prayed, "O Lord, I cannot say these words

because there is someone on earth whom I love." A conflict followed while he remained on his knees, but eventually he was able to say, "Lord, I will lay her aside. I am ready for her never to be mine."

Nee recalls, "At long last I was able to say the words of Psalm 73:25. I was in the second heaven, if not the third. On that day, February 13, 1922, when I laid aside my beloved, my heart was emptied of everything which had previously held me."

A decade passed before his prayers were answered. While Charity was studying at Yanjing University, Beijing, she made a firm commitment of faith. After graduating with an M.A. in English she moved to Shanghai and was baptized. Nee had by now commenced his ministry in this metropolis.

Thus it was that Watchman and Charity were married in Hangzhou in 1934. The preacher had just concluded a very fruitful conference. It was a good opportunity to "tie the knot." His mother, Heping, was present, as were his co-workers. Nee's mother pressed her son to get married while all his friends were near. But there was another important reason. An aunt of Charity's was bitterly opposed to the two getting married. As far as she was concerned a brilliant young lady with a promising career ahead of her was marrying a ne'er-do-well freelance preacher. The aunt tried to discredit Nee in a Shanghai newspaper, but he ignored the false charges and refused to respond to them.

During the early 1930s Nee had contact and a degree of fellowship with some Exclusive Brethren from London, England. He found himself in accord with much of their teaching. They were non-denominational, they were striving to recover the simplicity of the early church and they observed the Lord's supper weekly. But when Nee visited Britain he also had fellowship with believers outside these Exclusive Brethren assemblies—the China Inland Mission, the Keswick Convention and the Honor Oak Fellowship

*Watchman Nee, founder of the Little Flock movement, married
Charity Zhang on October 19, 1934 in Hangzhou*

in south London. The Brethren strongly disapproved of these associations.

After he had returned to his work in China he was surprised to receive a letter in 1935 from the Brethren leaders in Britain announcing that they had decided to sever all connection with his assemblies in China. At this time Watchman and Charity went to Yantai for a rest. In this port revival meetings were being held. Here he received teaching that brought him the deep measure of spiritual renewal which he needed. Into his preaching came a new emphasis on the work of the Holy Spirit. He said, "In prayer I feel that I am being filled by the Holy Spirit and his power descending on me."

In 1938, Nee found a new centre for spiritual help and fellowship. He formed close links with the Honor Oak Fellowship in south London and a firm friendship with Rev. Austin Sparks, its pastor. From him he learned the teaching on the tripartite nature of man. The two men attended the Keswick Convention together. Nee was called upon to pray for China and to take part in a large united communion service.

Nee returned to China at the time when the Sino-Japanese War was spreading over a large area of his country. His house in Shanghai was destroyed by Japanese bombs. The loose polity of the Little Flock was being severely tested. He had rejected the normal structures of the Western churches in China, which consisted of local church, a district council and a synod. He had sent some two hundred workers to new areas in China to pioneer assemblies and move on as soon as possible to commence further ones. But the devastations of war disrupted normal life and hindered the growth of the assemblies for which he had hoped. There was now increasing poverty so that local financial support for these pioneers was quite inadequate. He had consistently taught his workers to "look to God for divine supply." This he had strongly advocated in his book *Concerning our Missions*.[8] But, whatever the theory, the hard fact was that the workers of the Little Flock were suffering from insufficient support.

This situation led to Nee making a decision which he later admitted was a serious misjudgment. That decision set in motion a chain of events that would cast a dark shadow over his public ministry as a preacher. His response to this financial crisis was to join his brother Huaizu in his CBC Laboratories in Shanghai. Nee's co-workers in the ministry were employed as company representatives. The profits of the company were to go towards the support of his 200 workers throughout the country.

Soon this work in the pharmaceutical company absorbed more and more of Nee's time, and his preaching ministry suffered. With the escalation of the war the factory was moved to Chongqing in southwest China. For two and a half years the preacher travelled back and forth between the Chongqing factory and the Shanghai assembly. It was not long before the Shanghai elders, themselves the products of his own careful instruction, stopped him from preaching. What he was now doing was a contradiction of what he had himself taught over the years. In addition to his absorption in business affairs his spiritual life had become lax, and he was slipping from his one-time close walk with the Lord.

In 1947, soon after the end of the Sino-Japanese War, Watchman Nee made a full confession to his Shanghai elders and deacons, and a year later was allowed to preach again. During the interim he had preached from time to time in Chongqing and Fuzhou, away from the control and discipline of the elders in Shanghai, and perhaps unbeknownst to them.

At this time of Nee's restoration Stephen Kaung, a Little Flock worker, wrote to Rev. Austin Sparks, then in Scotland. The letter is dated April 16, 1947:

> I think that you will be glad to know that Brother Nee may return to our midst and be received at any moment. Brother

8 Also known as *The Normal Christian Church Life* (1939).

Nee's case was a mortal wound to us. Objections to his coming back have been gradually eliminated. From all observations hearts are ready, both Brother Nee's and those of the brethren. We are waiting for the right moment.

Over a year later Watchman Nee was preaching again. He did so with fresh zest, and the small building became dangerously full. James Chen tells us:

When Nee spoke for the first time there was the sound of weeping. Many workers confessed their sins and forgave one another. All divisions, difficulties and differences of opinion were swept away. Each member without reserve gave up himself and his possessions [to the Lord].

In 1948, a new hall in Nanyang Road seating 4,000 was completed. His new theme to his congregation now was the "handing over" of themselves and their belongings to the church, as exemplified in Acts 4:32. Hundreds obeyed and handed over their businesses, jewellery and ornaments to the church.

It was the last year of complete religious freedom in China, and what was brought in, in response to Nee's preaching, was carefully used to finance an ambitious "evangelism-by-migration" programme. Groups of believers were sent with their families to distant provinces to establish new assemblies, and when departing they were given sufficient funds for three months, after which time they were expected to support themselves as "tent makers." Nee had a vision of China being evangelized in this way within fifteen years. He acquired a property in Guling where intensive training courses were given to the key workers.

Meanwhile the civil war in China between the Nationalists and the Communists was drawing to its end. By early 1949, Mao Zedong had captured Tianjin, Beijing and Nanjing. This victory was bad news for the Little Flock, who had shown more confidence in the Nationalists, in spite of their complete failure to control inflation and to improve the critical conditions under which the farmers, who were the bulk of the population, were living. In 1950, Watchman Nee, visiting Hong Kong, had the opportunity to remain there and thus avoid conflict with the new regime. His friends pleaded with him not to return to mainland China, but he was convinced that his duty was to share in the sufferings facing his fellow Christians, and so he returned.

Nee was aware that he, together with many other Christians, would soon be suffering for their faith. And so he wrote a hymn based on Galatians 6:17 ("I bear in my body the marks of the Lord Jesus Christ") in which Christ is saying:

> *Why have you no marks?*
> *I was persecuted and hung alone on the Tree,*
> *Surrounded with coldness, cruelty and pride.*
> *I was hurt by rod, spear and nails,*
> *Why have you no marks?* [9]

Soon there followed "Accusation Meetings" in the main cities of China and the "Five Antis" drive (anti-bribery, anti-tax evasion, anti-theft of state property, anti-cheating on government contracts and anti-stealing of economic information). On April 10, 1952 Nee, aged 49, was arrested on all these five charges and held in prison until 1956, when he was brought before the Shanghai Higher People's Court. He was accused of having supported the imperialists, having backed the Nationalist regime, corrupting youth and acting licentiously. Nee was sentenced to imprisonment for fifteen years, of which he had already served four. In the same period Charity was arrested, imprisoned and then released in 1957 on account of her deteriorating health.

Watchman Nee was sent to the Shanghai Tilan Bridge Prison,

---

[9] From the *New Selection of Hymns for the Little Flock*, No. 59, verse 2.

and placed in a cell nine feet by four and a half feet, in which was a wooden platform on which to sleep. Upon her own release, Charity was able to see him regularly under supervision, bringing with her food and clothes for him. With the harsh conditions at this prison Nee's health eventually deteriorated, and his weight dropped to less than 100 pounds. He had a time in the prison hospital suffering from coronary ischaemia.

———

A brighter side to the story is that a year after his move to the small prison cell, a book was published in Bombay, *The Normal Christian Life*, which was an English translation of his earlier addresses at conferences in Shanghai and Hangzhou. In it Nee expounds the book of Romans. This has since been published in thirty languages and over a million copies have been sold. Like the apostle Paul who was imprisoned in the first century, Nee's voice was silenced by authorities but his messages were being read abroad, bringing blessing to their readers.

Following the publication of *The Normal Christian Life* was Nee's exposition of Ephesians under the title *Sit, Walk, Stand*. This has since been published in twenty-two languages, and close to a million copies have been sold. Altogether over fifty books of Nee's sermons, which had been taken down in shorthand at church conferences by Nee's close colleague, Ruth Li (Li Yuanru) have been published.

The preacher's burden expressed in these books was that the living of a holy and Spirit-filled life should be the norm for every Christian. But it would be a mistake to associate Watchman Nee solely with the theme of holiness. His addresses touched on every aspect of the Christian life. In a lesser-read book of his sermons Nee stresses that the Christian should have a high spiritual view of every part of his life, not just the occasions when he is publicly performing a service in the church. In this book he says, "All work ought to be service to God. If we are serving God, if we are ministering to the Lord, then we are priests indeed."[10]

In this he was echoing the well-known words of Horatius Bonar a century earlier:

> *So shall no part of day or night*
> *From sacredness be free.*
> *But all my life, in every step*
> *Be fellowship with Thee.*

His two most widely read books, already mentioned, have been read with blessing by Christians of many denominations. For them the reading of these devotional books have been spiritual landmarks in their lives. No doubt together with other spiritual classics these two books—*The Normal Christian Life* and *Sit, Walk, Stand*—will continue to be on the bookshelves of Christians for many generations to come.

In 1966, the ten-year long Cultural Revolution began, during which thousands of Christians suffered indescribable hardships. Charity was jailed as an "anti-revolutionary." She was put in a small room by the Red Guards, interrogated and severely tortured. Her relatives, waiting outside for her, could hear the lashings of a leather whip amid sounds of threats and abuse. When she emerged from the torture chamber her face was scarred and her eyes swollen. During that period she and two of her sisters were forced to walk down the street wearing dunce caps and heavy boards around their necks on which were insulting slogans.

The main purpose of the Red Guards was to force the three women to deny their faith in Christ, but they bore their harsh treatment in silence and dignity. Finally, their tormentors shouted at them, "Do you still believe in Jesus?" to which all three replied

10 Watchman Nee, *God's Work* (New York: Christian Fellowship Publishers, 1974), 64.

in the affirmative. The Red Guards then proceeded to throw shoes and other objects at them and called out, "Your obstinacy will send you to God sooner than you expect."

For Watchman Nee the year 1967 brought with it the prospect of release, having served his fifteen-year prison sentence. However, the authorities stipulated that he could only be freed if he denied his faith, but the preacher would not budge. Two hardened criminals were then placed in his cell with specific instructions to use every kind of violence possible to compel him to give up his faith. Nee suffered indescribable pain at the hands of these two thugs, but refused to deny his Master.

When his prison term expired he was secretly transferred to the Qing Dong Reform-through-Labour Farm in Qingpu County on the outskirts of Shanghai. Charity was allowed to visit him here on one occasion. For a few months there was no information as to his whereabouts, and then his wife learned that he had been sent to the dreaded Baimaoling Reform-through-Labour Farm, up in the mountains of Anhui province. Although the living conditions for the prisoners at this farm were tough and primitive, Nee found consolation and strength in his environment, for he wrote to his eldest sister, "Here the mountains are beautiful and the water clear."

On November 7, 1971 Charity Zhang passed away after months of suffering from high blood pressure and heart disease. Her family delayed breaking the sad news to Nee by letter, knowing that his health was poor. During the long years in prison Watchman Nee's strong desire had been that he would be released while Charity was still alive. As he lay awake on his hard bed he realized, with much regret, that his wife had suffered loneliness when he was travelling around China and overseas, addressing conferences. They had only been together for relatively short periods during their married life. He resolved that he would make it up to her if he had this opportunity. He would serve her, wait on her and do all he could to give her a restful retirement in

Watchman Nee was arrested on April 10, 1952, accused of having
supported the imperialists, having backed the Nationalist regime,
corrupting youth and acting licentiously. He remained in captivity
until his death on May 30, 1972 while en route to a hospital,
near the Baimaoling Reform-through-Labour Farm,
Anhui province, to treat a critical heart condition.
He remained faithful to the end.

their closing years together. But it was not to be.

Sooner or later Charity's family had to break the sad news to the distant prisoner. From information which his cellmates gave after his death Nee was in deep sorrow for many days. He was seen to be in prayer for many hours at a time.

On May 22, 1972 Nee wrote a coded letter to his sister-in-law in Beijing, in which he assured her that "my joy is full." Obviously his reference to John 15:11 indicated that his faith was still unshaken, although the authorities had been asserting that the preacher had abandoned his faith while in prison.

Nee was aware that with his suffering from angina pectora he was daily getting weaker. His letters written during May 1972 reveal his strong desire to die among his own people. In one letter he said, "I deeply long to return to my own relatives and be with them, just as a falling leaf returns to its roots...I am seeking a final resting place."

On May 30, 1972, with a critical heart condition and in urgent need of medical treatment, Nee was placed on a tractor to go to the prison hospital some twelve miles away. The prisoner was too weak to travel along the rough and bumpy mountain road, and as the tractor jolted to the discomfort of the frail and dying passenger, Watchman Nee died *en route*.

Nee had known that death was imminent, for after his passing a note was found under his pillow written in his weak and shaky handwriting:

> Christ is the Son of God. He died as the Redeemer for the sins of humankind, and was raised up from the dead after three days. This is the most important fact in the world. I shall die believing in Christ. Ni Tuosheng.

The authorities wanted to advise the public that the preacher had died without a Christian faith. But in this crumpled piece of paper was a clear refutation of such a suggestion. When one of

Charity's sisters and her daughter visited the farm prison after his death the cadre in charge showed them his ashes and allowed them to see this crumpled piece of paper, the words of which they memorized. During this visit a friendly fellow prisoner of Nee's told the two women, with tears in his eyes, that not long after Nee's death he himself had personally come to faith in Christ.

Nee's ashes together with those of Charity Zhang lie in Suzhou, west of Shanghai.

The writer of the Letter to the Hebrews describes the fidelity, amid intense suffering, of the Heroes of the Faith in these words:

> From being weaklings they became strong men and mighty warriors…Some…were tortured and refused to be ransomed, because they wanted to deserve a more honourable resurrection in the world to come. Others were exposed to the test of public mockery and flogging, and to the torture of being left bound in prison…They lived as vagrants in the desert, on the mountains, or in caves or holes in the ground (Hebrews 11:34–37, J.B. PHILLIPS).

Nee was one such hero of the faith.

4

范培基
FAN PEIJI

1917–1987

The preacher/artist who had to make busts of Chairman Mao

> I am a knife in the hands of the Lord. A knife can either
> be kept sharp and be used or get rusty and be discarded.
> —*words spoken by Fan Peiji, when the opportunity arose to
> preach the gospel again in China in 1979*

The teacher was lecturing to his large middle school class on the
Chinese classics. Fan Peiji was doodling on a much-used scrap of
paper while listening intently to the talk. But it was doodling
with a difference. He was writing over and over again in his best
classical style three Chinese characters—Kong Fuzi—the three
characters for Confucius.

Between writing sentences on the blackboard the teacher
walked slowly up and down the aisles of the classroom. As he
passed young Fan's desk he slowed down. While continuing to
give his lecture he glanced at the student's scribblings and said to
himself prophetically, "Fan will be a calligrapher one day." He
was to take every opportunity to encourage this bright student to
develop his obvious talent.

Fan Peiji, like the other pupils in his class, had come to school
with articles which are called "the four treasures of the room of

literature"—a brush, a brush stand, a block of ink and a stone ink slab. With his brush he was writing characters over and over on the cheap paper until it disintegrated.

The Yi Wen Middle School in Yantai, on the coast of Shandong, was a large school run by the American Presbyterian mission. It had 400 students and its curriculum included both the Chinese classics and modern literature, as well as the reading and writing of English. At its head was the popular William Booth, a kind and courteous missionary who spoke Chinese fluently and rode to school each day on a bicycle. Booth served the school for thirty-nine years, twenty years of which he was the school principal. Booth was assisted by the efficient Li Lan-jie, the dean of the school, who had come to Yantai after a professorship in the Hangzhou University.

As we have already noted, at the end of the 1920s there was political unrest throughout China. This included banditry, fighting between warlords competing for spheres of influence and widespread poverty, particularly among the peasants. Young Fan witnessed street fights in the port of Yantai between the Northeast Clique and the Hebei/Shandong Clique. Fortunately the local Chamber of Commerce intervened and raised sufficient funds to appease both rival groups, so that commerce and education were not further disturbed.

Fan participated in many of the school's activities. William Booth and Mr. Li wisely allowed the student body to observe important dates in the Chinese calendar. There was the Fruit Tree Blossom Festival, the annual intermural Sports Day, and Republic Day on October 10 (the Double Tenth), when the students marched in their uniforms and sang patriotic songs. Every Monday morning there was a memorial ceremony in honour of Dr. Sun Yat Sen (Sun Zhongshan), the founder of the Republic of China.

There were also meetings on the campus that supported the leadership of Chiang Kai Shek (Jiang Jieshi), and meetings advocating support for the newly formed Communist party. In later years some of the graduates of Yi Wen were to become leaders of the Kuomintang and some of the Communist party. Young Fan took little interest in these political activities at the school. He was quiet, industrious, and studied hard at all his subjects, and was usually the highest in his class. In his spare time he practised calligraphy. If he wrote an essay he would take pride in printing the title and subject in carefully shaped characters.

Fan Peiji was born in 1917 in the village of Henan in the district of Haiyang in northeast Shandong. It was a humble home amid the brown hills and maize fields of that area of the country. He was the first child in the family, and being a boy his arrival was greeted with much approval. His mother died when he was only three and he grew up unable to remember anything about her. His father re-married and three girls were born to this second marriage.

His stepmother was kind to him and brought him up well with her three daughters, but it was from his grandmother in this traditional three-generation household that he received the love and affection which he needed in those formative years.

Life was not easy for Peiji's father, Fan Zhenyu, who ran a small farm with his brother Fan Zhentai. There were regular periods of drought that made farming quite unprofitable. Food was often too scarce to feed his large family adequately. To supplement his low income Fan Zhenyu worked as a practitioner in traditional Chinese medicine. And in the evenings he also sat by his kerosene lamp making hats that were sold at the local market.

Fan Zhenyu was a humble Christian believer. Christianity had first come to this part of Shandong about 1870, when Hunter Corbett, a Presbyterian missionary, began travelling regularly to eastern Shandong from Yantai. He would come on a pushcart loaded with food and religious books and assisted by a Chinese helper. In the early pioneering days these visits were fraught with danger, for Corbett was often attacked and stoned, and any who responded to his preaching would be beaten up by the local inhabitants and sometimes even have their homes destroyed. The local populace did not want the so-called Jesus doctrine to take root in their environs.

But tragedy struck the province of Shandong in 1876. There was an excessively long drought resulting in widespread crop failure, and thousands of peasants died of hunger and malnutrition. Corbett, just back from furlough in the United States, travelled to nearby Jimo and managed to bring relief to thousands of sufferers.

One of the effects of this devastating famine, in which millions in the four northern provinces died, was that there was a changed attitude to foreign missionaries. No longer were they seen as a threat to their way of life. Rather, they were now considered trustworthy friends. Corbett travelled across the northern part of Shandong each spring and autumn, faithfully planting the seeds of the gospel wherever he went. His route included Fushan, Muping, Qixia, Laiyang, Haiyang and Jimo. During the latter part of the nineteenth century and early twentieth century village churches sprang up along this route, and with each church a village school was opened.

At the turn of the century, when the Boxers were rampaging through the province, it is said that the farmers of eastern Shandong sent an urgent message to them, "Do not kill or harm Corbett." Before his death at the age of eighty-five, the Chinese Imperial Court awarded him the Double Dragon Medal, the highest civilian honour.

Chu Chengmin later said of him, "Hunter Corbett, though born in the United States, was indeed one of us, and will be remembered by all those who knew him and his good work throughout the northeastern part of Shandong province."

Within a few years of the 1876–1878 famine, members of the Fan clan professed faith in Christ. Dr. Corbett regularly visited their humble home in later years and suggested that young Fan

Peiji should proceed from the primary school at Laiyang to the mission's middle school in Yantai.

Just at the time when Fan graduated from the Yi Wen Middle School a spiritual movement was taking place in the churches and mission schools throughout Shandong. In 1930 the National Christian Council had launched a Five Year Forward Movement, the motto of which was "Revive Thy church, O Lord, beginning with me." Coinciding with that was a spontaneous movement which came to be called the "Shandong Revival." Addresses given by Miss Marie Monsen, a Norwegian Lutheran missionary, had brought revival and renewal among the missionary community and among the Chinese pastors, workers and church members.

In the wake of her stirring meetings came Dr. John Sung (Song Shangjie).[1] Fan Peiji heard him one day in a crowded meeting in Yantai and was arrested by his powerful preaching. Sung was direct and blunt, and he fearlessly attacked formal religion and hypocrisy. He enlivened his messages with suitable gestures that brought home effectively the truths that he was preaching. He called for confession and restitution, and appealed for young people to dedicate their whole lives to the service of Jesus Christ.

Fan had been brought up in a Christian home. He had received his education both in Laiyang and Yantai in Christian schools, and had therefore received regular instruction in spiritual things. It was while listening to this Spirit-filled preacher that he realized that "God has no spiritual grandchildren." There must come a day in a person's life when, however religious his environment may be, he makes a personal commitment to Jesus Christ.

When these special meetings in Yantai were over Fan knew that there was only one thing which God wanted him to do—to preach the Gospel and win his fellow countrymen for Christ.

---

[1] On the life of John Sung (1901–1944), see Leslie T. Lyall, *John Sung: Flame for God in the Far East* (5th ed. Chicago: Moody Press, 1964).

Referring to this decision, he wrote to me half a century later:

> I was converted at one of Sung's special meetings and
> offered myself for Christian service. Now as I look back I
> realize how much God used him to do an important work
> of reviving the Chinese church, which was able to stand up
> in the trying times ahead, and leading up to the wonderful
> harvest of the present time.

Fan made enquiries as to where he could receive training for
the ministry, and was told about the China Inland Mission Bible
School in Hangzhou in central China. He applied and was
accepted, and travelled south to Shanghai and on to Hangzhou.
In settling into his new life in these new surroundings the young
student experienced culture shock.

Instead of the flat roofs of the north he saw the thatched roofs
of Zhejiang. Not far from the Bible school was the famous West
Lake, which was more beautiful than anything he had seen in his
native Shandong. Moreover, Hangzhou was far more modern than
Yantai. The churches seemed to be different. Christian missionaries
had come to these parts some thirty years before they came to
Shandong and so the congregations were more mature and self-
supporting. John Sung had also had a city-wide mission here and the
fruits of this were clearly evident. Finally, there was the challenge
of attuning his northern speech to local ways of speaking.

There were about seventy students at the Bible school, half of
them men and half of them women. Students with a limited
education took the school's short-term Bible training course, while
the majority with a better education took the long-term Bible
training course. The latter syllabus was just what Fan was wanting.

Life at the Bible school was very full. The daily routine
required that the students be disciplined and prompt. Howard
Cliff, my father, and Pastor Liu Tiande gave the students a
systematic study of the Bible, as well as a training programme of

*Fan Peiji received his pastoral training at the China Inland Mission
Bible School in Hangzhou, central China*

practical work. The aim of the school was not to turn out graduates with a theoretical knowledge of the Bible, but to prepare young men and women to be leaders of the church in China in all aspects of its witness.

At first the students could not understand each other very well. Some came from Jiangsu, some from Anhui, others from Jiangxi, with the majority coming from Zhejiang. In those days the learning of the official Mandarin (*pu tong hua*) was not compulsory in the schools. But all the dialects used the same characters, even though they pronounced them differently. Howard Cliff spoke Mandarin well, but he had to write the points of his lecture on the blackboard so that all in the class could understand. Fan learned the local dialect quickly, and eagerly took notes at the classes. At eighteen he was the youngest student in the Bible school, but he always came first in tests and examinations. The school often made use of his skills in calligraphy for the making of banners and the printing of programmes.

The school assembly room served as the church for the community each Sunday. He became increasingly confident in taking part in the services as well as in leading morning prayers at the Bible school during the week. After the morning service each Sunday the students went by bicycle to scattered parts of Hangzhou to carry out various forms of Christian witness. Some conducted open-air services, while others visited local prisons. Still others went from bed to bed in mission hospitals and spoke to the patients about the love of Christ.

When holidays came the students went to their homes and assisted in their local churches. Sometimes problems arose during the vacation. One student, upon returning to school, confessed to the Chinese principal that during his holidays he had taken part in an idol procession. The principal spoke to him about the spiritual principles involved in this action, and the student acknowledged his sin and was allowed to continue his studies.

There were two students at Hangzhou who came from the

Yantai area. Besides Fan there was another student called Liu Jianchiu. They would travel together for the thousand-mile journey to the north, where they were eager to be able to assist in their home churches. I recall one of these holidays. I was playing in the quadrangle of the Boys' School in Yantai, and was surprised to be told to go to the headmaster's study. There with Mr. P.A. Bruce was Fan Peiji waiting for me with his friendly smile. He had a parcel of food for me from my parents in Hangzhou.

In 1938, Fan finished his two-year course at the CIM Bible School. He graduated with distinctions in all his subjects, and was pleased to receive his diploma from Howard Cliff, who had always regarded him as a student of great promise. At this time an opportunity for service came to work on a "Gospel Boat," which plied its way up and down the Suzhou River. Fan's ear was now attuned to the various dialects of central China. As the boat threaded its way down the river in the Suzhou area, the young graduate and his co-workers took every opportunity to preach the gospel to the crowds at the riverside.

Then a chance to do more advanced theological studies opened up for him. Fan was accepted to study at the well-known China Bible Seminary in Jiangwan, on the outskirts of Shanghai. The seminary had a reputation for offering good training and sound scholarship. Many of its past graduates were now leaders in the church in China. It had a strong missionary emphasis, and some of its former scholars were doing effective pioneering work in difficult fields in northwest and southwest China.

At the China Bible Seminary Fan came under the rich expositions of David Yang (Yang Shaotang), who inspired him to preach verse by verse from the Bible. Yang's emphasis on the work of the Holy Spirit in the believer's life also left an indelible mark on the young student. Yang had been brought up in Shanxi province, and in 1934 had formed a Spiritual Action Team (*Ling Gong Tuan*) there. He had constructed some modest buildings in which two dozen young men and women at a time were given careful instruction. The aim of this small centre was to equip Christian workers spiritually for their future service for Christ. In 1939, Japanese soldiers burned down the buildings and forced the team to disband. When Yang moved to Shanghai to teach at the seminary there he maintained the same spiritual emphasis on the importance of the filling of the Spirit.

A friendship developed between Yang and Fan, so much so that when Yang was invited to be pastor of the Huang Ni Guang church in Nanjing in addition to his lecturing work, he invited young Fan to preach for him in Nanjing when he was away. Yang, as both pastor in Nanjing and lecturer in Shanghai, had to travel back and forth, and was glad to enlist Fan Peiji's help in maintaining the preaching ministry.

But Fan's time at the seminary was important in another way, for it was there that he met a female student, Yang Yunxiou, who was to become his wife. The two found that they had much in common. They were both from Shandong province; both had been educated in mission schools there; and both had been called into Christian service through the preaching of John Sung. In the same period of time when Fan had listened to Sung preaching in Yantai, Yang had attended his services in Weifang and had also committed herself to God's service. Lastly, they both had strong connections with the China Inland Mission.

Yang Yunxiou was born in Weifang and was brought up by her grandmother in Qingzhou. The latter had been a devout Buddhist. She had inherited some valuable property and was considerably better off than the people around her. But her life was filled with dissatisfaction. There was an aching void which money could not buy. A protracted drought had come to the area where she lived, and she was planning to go to the local temple to pray for rain. But her maid was a Christian, and pressed her to go to church and pray to the true God. She went to the Baptist church, where she was converted, baptized and became active in church meetings.

Yang's grandmother became a changed person, and her friends

noticed that she was now happy and contented. She used her property in Qingzhou to build a home for the needy. Many widows and orphans found shelter and love here. Christian services were held here daily, and the tenants were encouraged to help grow the food that they needed. Under her leadership this home became a small self-contained community.

Another result of the grandmother's conversion was that she wanted to dedicate Yang to the Lord for his service. She resolved to arrange a Christian education for her, and so Yang studied at the Baptist school, and then did further studies at the Presbyterian school in Weifang. The teachers at the Qingzhou school made a great impression on the young student, and one Scottish lady teacher later kept in touch with her while she was studying in Shanghai.

Fan and Yang thus became engaged, though it would be a further two years before they were married.

Soon after Fan's graduation from the CIM Bible School he received a letter from his former principal, Howard Cliff. Howard and Mary Cliff were now working in Henan. Would he join them in their work of running short-term Bible schools in various centres of the province? This was just the kind of work to which he seemed suited, and soon he left Shanghai to live in Luohe in south Henan.

The province was subject to Japanese air raids, and there were also regular skirmishes between government troops and the 8th Route Army. The common people were finding it increasingly difficult to continue doing their normal work, and it was hard to support and feed their families. The roads were rough and public transportation very poor. The evangelistic and training work of missionaries was also becoming difficult to maintain. There was a sense of urgency that Chinese workers had to be trained to preach and teach in case the Western missionaries were forced to evacuate. The clouds were darkening on the political horizon. But Howard and Mary Cliff and Fan Peiji were determined to redeem the time and give suitable training as urgently and effectively as possible.

Using Luohe as a base, the trio went in a circle counter-clockwise to Sheqi, Huangchuan, Zhoukou and Fuyang (just over the border in Anhui), spending a few months at each place and then moving on to the next stop. Writing to me about this work forty years later, Fan recalled an incident that he said he would never forget:

> In the winter of 1941 Mr. Cliff and I were working together in Bible school work. He and I both taught Bible subjects, and Mrs. Cliff taught music and hymns. We were leaving Henan and going to Anhui. Halfway there something happened which I shall never forget. It was during the Japanese War, and the roads were very bad, and we had no vehicle for transport.
>
> Mrs. Cliff was in a pushcart, and Mr. Cliff and I followed on bicycles. Today this journey would only take a few hours, but this one took three days. We spent the night in a village inn. During the night bandits stole the baggage in the cart. Mrs. Cliff was very quiet. Her first words were, "Thank God we are all safe." But all her belongings had been stolen. We continued the second day of the journey to our destination as though nothing had happened. They were in complete peace and serenity. How can one not be moved in recalling this?

Fan spent two happy years travelling to each of the five centres where the short-term Bible schools were held for a few months in each place. But the advance of the Japanese westwards from the coast forced Howard and Mary Cliff to withdraw from teaching to spend time in prayer about the future. Their three children at school in Yantai would in all likelihood be forced into a Japanese internment camp with the other children of missionaries. It was surely their parental duty to settle in a Western country and prepare a home for them to go to when the war ended, whenever that would be. And so it was during 1942 that the two missionaries left Henan and settled in South Africa.

It was time for Fan Peiji to make another change of work. For two years he had been engaged to Yang Yunxiou, who was now working with the CIM in Jiangxi province. The two were married in the home of the bride's grandmother in Qingzhou. Then they proceeded to Zhoukou to help in a CIM Bible school. Bravely they continued serving their Lord amid the dangerous conditions of the war. Twice they went on holiday to Mrs. Fan's home, where her grandmother lived. Although they needed a rest from their work they took the daily services at the grandmother's home for the needy, and won the hearts of the children in the home.

But when it became impossible to maintain the work in Zhoukou and the Bible School had to be closed down due to the advancing Japanese armies, they returned to their native Shandong. They settled in Qingzhou. It was in an area of the province where the British Baptists had established a strong work, and so Pastor Fan formed a small Baptist church. Later they learned that Howard and Mary's three children were only forty miles away in Weifang, where 1,800 "enemy subjects" of the Japanese were in an internment camp.

For two years, in an area where the Japanese were firmly in control, Pastor and Mrs. Fan worked hard to build a church in this very difficult situation. Then came the welcome news that the Japanese had surrendered and their long period of occupation was coming to an end. The couple was now asked to open a Bible school in Yidu county, where they had been working. For a year they did this important work. In 1947 they were invited to teach in the Hua Dong Bible School in Suzhou, Jiangsu province.

In 1948, Fan's old friend David Yang (Yang Shaotang) invited him to become his assistant at the Huang Ni Guang church in Nanjing, where he had frequently preached in his student days. Yang Shaotang had been given additional responsibilities at the China Bible Seminary, and needed assistance in maintaining the church in Nanjing, which had grown considerably under his dynamic preaching. Fan was happy to accept and moved with his family to Nanjing, where he was to stay for the remaining four decades of his life. He had worked in Jiangsu, Henan and Shandong, but henceforth his work for the Lord would be in the important capital of Nanjing.

The bitter civil war in China was clearly nearing its end. The authority of the central government was crumbling, and city after city fell to the Communists. On October 1, 1949, soon after Fan's arrival with his family in Nanjing, Mao Zedong declared the inauguration of the People's Republic of China from the Gate of Heavenly Peace in Tiananmen Square. After all the oppression and exploitation of past years China was promised a new deal. During their steady advance towards Beijing the Communists had assured the public that they would never interfere with religious activities.

But many Christians were apprehensive. Some pastors had left the country to serve congregations elsewhere. One of Fan's former classmates, now pastoring a church in Singapore, had invited him to join him as co-pastor there before the Communists took control. But, apart from the fact that Fan could not speak the dialect of the church members, he felt strongly that he could not abandon his flock in Nanjing.

In the first few months after "Liberation" Pastor Fan was able to continue his normal ministry of preaching and training. Church life in China proceeded, initially, without change. Soon, however, the real plans of the new regime became evident. Zhou Enlai began pressing the church leaders to rid themselves of all "imperialist influences." By 1951 all missionaries had left or been expelled from the country.

David Yang was away from the Nanjing church more and more frequently. Not only was he working hard as a lecturer at the China Bible Seminary, but he was addressing well-attended conferences and student gatherings in many centres. The church members at Huang Ni Guang church were enjoying the expositions

of Fan, the assistant minister. With the rapidly changing circumstances in the country Fan Peiji had a busy programme. In
addition to taking services on Sunday and meetings during the
week, including youth fellowship, prayer meeting and evangelistic
work among children, he had to spend much time counselling his
flock, praying with them and helping them to make sound
decisions in light of the sweeping changes in China.

The first experience which Fan had of the severity of the new
regime was in 1950, not long after "Liberation." He had been
speaking at some meetings in Shandong. On his way home to
Nanjing he gave out some religious tracts to his fellow passengers
on the train. He was arrested and imprisoned for ten days, during
which time the authorities tried to prove that he was a "dangerous
reactionary." There was one factor that was in his favour. His
family background was not "capitalist"—his father had been a
peasant farmer. He was asked about his attitude to the recently
formed Three Self Patriotic Movement. Fortunately at this stage he
knew little about this new organization, and so he could truthfully
say that he had not yet formulated his ideas about it.

For China's Christians, the 1950s were a prolonged nightmare.
"Accusation Meetings" were held in all the principal cities.
Pastors were falsely accused by their colleagues and sent to
"reform-through-labour" camps for some twenty years. Some
committed suicide and others lost their faith altogether. To avoid
trouble with the authorities one had to use a degree of subtlety.
Fan, after hours of angry interrogation and cross-examination,
found a way out of this pressure to "accuse" by listing the mistakes
of certain leaders who had left the country or who had died. By
this means no one was hurt, and he had saved himself from
further demands.

One day Fan's senior colleague Yang was given a public trial in
his home church in Nanjing. Among the false charges made
against him was one made by a former female colleague at the
CIM Bible School with regard to his past loyalties. The crowds

cheered and shouted for his death. Yang was visibly shocked and hurt. The result of the trial was that he was ejected from his pastorate. He then moved to Shanghai to continue his work at the seminary. There Yang realized that in order to have any opportunity to preach and teach he would have to posture himself as a nominal supporter of the TSPM. In 1958 he was appointed the Assistant Secretary of the Shanghai Three Self Committee. Circumstances had forced him to make a show of interest in this organization.

Yang's departure meant that Fan had more work and responsibility in the church, and the harsh treatment which his senior colleague had received was a reminder to him that his turn might be next. In the meantime he resolved to do his work to the utmost of his ability.

But a year later Fan had to reluctantly make a change. Churches throughout China were closed and taken over for government use, and pastors were forced to find other employment. All the churches in Nanjing were forced to merge and the Christians had to meet in one building; this included the Huang Ni Guang church. As Fan Peiji was a self-taught artist and calligrapher, he found employment in the Nanjing Art and Advertising Company. His work was to design advertisements for the company, and this new task he did with some enjoyment. Here he found expression for his love of calligraphy, writing advertisements in various styles of character. This work was creative, and he was free from the pressures which were placed on pastors in those years.

From 1959 to 1979 he worked for the company. Although his heart was in preaching the gospel, there was a degree of relief in no longer being involved in the tensions and acrimony of church life. He was glad to give expression to his lifelong love of painting. But he was still a pastor. Church members visited his home in twos and threes. The family's meagre meals were shared with them. His people needed spiritual advice for the critical days in which they found themselves. They also needed practical help.

The pastor wrote letters for them because of their limited education, and helped them to complete application forms.

Throughout China Christians were going through a time of testing and sifting. In Nanjing, too, the believers went through a fiery trial of their faith. Fan found that some of his sheep had turned against him. He had to be tight-lipped when they were around. Others kept silent—they were playing a safe game, afraid to speak out and admit their past links with the church. But, happily, some came closer than ever to him. His fellowship with them was of a depth and quality that he had not experienced before. When they knew that Fan needed encouragement they came around to assure him of their continued friendship.

In addition to all the pressures of the new regime Fan and his family had to struggle for survival. Fan had five children and in addition to them there was his mother-in-law to support—in all eight mouths to feed. During the so-called Great Leap Forward the country had a series of natural and economic disasters. His growing children had to eat the simplest food, and hunger was never far away. However, the family today recall that in spite of these acute shortages there was harmony and love between them. They had regular family prayers. Fan wrote the hymns out on pieces of paper and painted pictures around the characters to make it more attractive for the younger ones. Today Sheng, the youngest of the family recalls, "We children were taught the Christian faith throughout our youth, but it was done secretly to avoid any trouble."

During this period Fan applied to the authorities for a transfer to Xinjiang in northwest China. Perhaps in his mind was the hope that he might be able to get away from the constant harassment of being a pastor and in these faraway parts might be able to witness for Christ. But, not being in the good books of the government, his request was firmly refused.

In 1966, Mao's great proletarian Cultural Revolution, which was to last ten years, shook the very foundations of Chinese society. Many Communist leaders, who had been Mao's colleagues on the historic Long March thirty years earlier, were disgraced and purged, or put under house arrest. Writers, historians, educators, army officers, Party cadres and church leaders were publicly insulted and humiliated. Schools and colleges were closed down. What little education there was centred around the thoughts of Chairman Mao.

Mao dispatched thousands of young people as Red Guards into the cities to destroy all works of art, statues, paintings, crosses and crucifixes, Bibles and hymn books. Transport was paralyzed as eleven million Red Guards travelled to the big cities. Factory production was reduced because of strikes, interference from the young Red Guards and power struggles.

These young people forced pastors to wear dunce caps and walk down the main street wearing heavy boards on which there was written things like "running dog of the imperialists." The Red Guards wrought much destruction wherever they went. In later years Fan wrote to me, describing the Cultural Revolution as "ten years of riots, lawlessness, confusion and turmoil, and it caused incalculable harm and loss. Because I had been a preacher I suffered from the very beginning of this period, and could not do my normal work, or in fact any work at all. I could only do odd manual jobs here and there. I was constantly interrogated but, because they could find no proof of my being anti-revolutionary, they could not send me to prison."

The Cultural Revolution brought much suffering and humiliation to Fan and his family. He was publicly condemned as a "running dog of the imperialists." On his way to work the children in the neighbourhood would throw stones at him.

Then there was Yang, a carpenter, who was head of the local Revolutionary Committee. Passing Fan's home daily on his way to work, he took every opportunity to hurl abuse at him. One day when he passed he saw the pastor studying a large Chinese dictionary and shouted, "Other people here cannot afford such a large book." Later, when Yang was dying of cancer, he sent for the pastor, asked forgiveness for his harsh treatment, repented of his sins and died a believer.

As part of the programme of destruction of anything associated with culture or religion, Fan was instructed one day to take his treasured theological books, a collection built up over many years, to the Waste Paper Shop for the purpose of recycling. He had different translations of the Bible in Chinese, encyclopedias and commentaries, which he used regularly in preparing his sermons. The hardest book to part with was an ornate English Bible, which an American missionary had passed on to him when forced to leave China. It had beautiful coloured illustrations that Fan as a lover of art often gazed at. The pastor decided to cut off the attractive cover made of Jerusalem olive and take only the contents to the shop with his other valued books. The shopkeeper gave him 10 yuan for the paper, but no amount of money could have replaced these treasures from the past. He came home from the shop sickened and depressed at this cruel deprivation. One of the hard lessons of the Cultural Revolution was the constant reminder that whatever else he lost no one could deprive him of inner faith, tranquility and communion with his God.

Another cruel aspect of the Cultural Revolution for Pastor and Mrs. Fan was the fact that their five children suffered discrimination because they were part of a Christian family. They were disqualified from higher educational opportunities, and instead four of them were sent in their teens to state-run farms for "re-education." Fan Sheng recalled, "We sometimes complained about our handicaps, which kept us from going to university because we came from an 'anti-revolutionary' family. Father must have been hurt by our words."

All over China people were being sent out from the towns to work in the fields in the countryside. For Mao the mass production of grain was the nation's supreme priority. So it was that one of Fan's children, Fan Qin, left home to work on a labour farm in Lianyungang, a port in northern Jiangsu. Two of the other children, Fan Yong and Fan Xin, went away to labour on separate farms. The fourth, Fan Pu, took a long and tiring journey with hundreds of other students from Nanjing to the northwest desert in Xinjiang. Only the youngest, Fan Sheng, remained at home and worked as a barber. He had been refused training to become an electrician.

The darkest period of the Cultural Revolution was at the end of the 1960s. The great land of China was engulfed in darkness and insanity. Mao Zedong was exalted as God, and it became compulsory to worship him. Wall posters proclaimed, "Chairman Mao, you are the Red Sun in our hearts."

The cult of Maoism was forced on every citizen. Every family had to have a bust of Mao in their home to revere and honour. Whether a person worked in an office, factory, school or hospital it was necessary to stand in front of a statue or picture of Chairman Mao and read the Little Red Book, both at the beginning and the end of the day's work.

The worship ceremony required standing in front of some representation of Mao. A picture was regarded as only two-dimensional, whereas a statue or bust added a further dimension, and was therefore regarded as being more meaningful. This strange turn of events brought bulk orders to the Nanjing Art and Advertising Company. Business was now brisk. The firm already had a department for the making of plaster statues of famous people to stand in halls and public places. This was now greatly expanded. An unused exhibition hall was taken over and additional staff were transferred to this department. All workers had to work at least ten hours a day.

Fan Peiji had been enjoying his art work as a welcome diversion from the acrimonious political situation in the country. But now he had to work long hours in order to keep up with bulk orders, and often was not permitted to go home. Fan Sheng described this period to me:

I often had to go to his workshop to bring food to him. At that time he had been accused of being a "counter-revolutionary," of being "a running dog of the American imperialists" and of "helping foreigners to invade China with spiritual opium," and so on. Although he suffered a lot physically, he had peace in his mind. He told me that what the revolutionaries had said about him he had made a matter of prayer, and rested in the knowledge that God was his final judge.

Pastor Fan's task in the process of making statues and busts was to put the finishing touches to other people's work. With his chisels and tools he had to remedy any defects he could identify. There were life-size statues to be perfected, but the bulk of the work related to head-and-shoulder busts, which was all most peasants could afford to buy.

This could not have been a less congenial task for this humble servant of God. He had always preached that images should not be made and worshipped. Did not the fourth of the Ten Commandments teach: "You shall not make for yourself an idol in the form of anything in heaven above or on the earth beneath...You shall not bow down to them or worship them" (Exodus 20:4–5, NIV).

As Fan chiselled and filed, and added the finishing touches to these plaster models he prayed and knew in his heart that God understood his complex situation better than he did. Fan Sheng, who brought food regularly to his father during this period, told me:

> During this time my father grew spiritually. His faith in God was deepened and his powers of endurance increased. These experiences prepared him for the future ten-year period when he would be able to preach again. He emerged from the Cultural Revolution a stronger Christian.

At last in the mid-1970s the drastic activities of the Red Guards as well as of others in government service came to an end. The ten-year Cultural Revolution ended with the death of Mao Zedong. Soon afterwards Deng Xiaoping introduced economic and political reforms, reversing many of the harsh measures of the past. Pastors were released from prisons. Churches were re-opened for worship. Young people returned from working on distant farms. A degree of freedom returned and the common people were able to breathe more freely.

In 1979, Pastor Fan was able to return to his former work of preaching and teaching. In spite of all the acrimony and accusations of earlier years and the betrayal of workers by their colleagues, he was surprised to discover that the number of Christians now ran into thousands and thousands, and to find that the people were eager to hear the Word of God.

He later wrote to me recalling this time and said, "My faith was weak. I had never dared to think that the church in China would have the revival which it was experiencing. This is the result of the prayers of Christians throughout the world." The discovery of the growth of the church spurred him to catch up on the years that had been wasted. He resolved, "I have lost so much time. I must redouble my efforts for God."

The churches in Nanjing were re-opened in 1980, and Fan was happy to resume his preaching and teaching. He was officially ordained by the China Christian Council and became the senior pastor of the Shanxi Road Church. He had strong reservations about the integrity of the Three Self Patriotic Movement (with its degree of control by the government's Religious Affairs Bureau) which had been recently revived, but he recognized, as did many other pastors, that to exploit the new opportunities he would have to work within its auspices. He remarked to his family, "I am a knife in the hands of the Lord. A knife can either be kept sharp and be used or get rusty and be discarded." He was now sixty years old. He had been forced to relinquish his preaching

Pastor Fan Peiji after "Liberation"

ministry for eighteen years. For whatever years still remained he was going to give his all for the service of God.

With renewed zeal he planned his future programme of systematic Bible exposition. The church, which seated only 200 people, was soon full and overflowing. The authorities warned the pastor that he would be held responsible if there were any accidents during worship. Fan soon found the solution by arranging for services to be held on Saturday morning and three times on Sunday. As he wrote to me, "Because our work has been disturbed we must work doubly hard. The opportunities for the church in China are limitless. We must nurture and build up the church to ensure that it has a firm foundation. There are lots of sheep, but not enough shepherds."

Fan Peiji began to make plans to achieve this. He would revert to the strategy that Howard and Mary Cliff had used in Henan. Nanjing would become his base, and he would go to a chosen centre to lead a short-term Bible training course, so that ordinary peasants in the villages could learn how to serve in their local churches. He would then return to his base and plan the next study course. He wrote to me just after one such course:

> For six weeks I have been in Huaiyin conducting training classes. The syllabus covers the Pentateuch, Romans and 1 and 2 Corinthians. Because of the time factor the programme is very tight. One day is given to music and hymns. There are seven subjects altogether.
>
> Many of the students are from the villages, and their standard of education is very low. The average age is 28. Some are from Christian families, but most are new Christians. They have hearts full of the love of God. After the training they go back to the villages to be responsible for preaching the gospel in the services.
>
> There are many meeting places, and congregations vary from 100 to 1,000. In many of the villages churches are in the process of being built. Everyone takes part in the activities. I have been doing this kind of work for the past eight years. There are forty in this school.

And then he goes on to say, "At present the most difficult aspect of the work is that the harvest is ripe and the workers are so few."

In another letter he explained the workings of the post-denominational church in China. "The present situation of the church is that there are no denominational divisions. At our

Fan Peiji was the senior pastor of the Shanxi Road Church, Nanjing. He also ministered to the peasants in the surrounding villages.

Sunday services we follow a common order of worship. The basis of our belief is the Apostles' Creed, and the workers respect one another's viewpoints. We receive the people into church membership by baptism, which can be by immersion or sprinkling. We let the individual choose." He was fully supportive of this aspect of the China Christian Council's work—the elimination of the former denominations which had divided and confused the church's witness in China—though he was wary of the degree of government control over the life of the church.

In this new spirit of freedom and opportunity Fan responded to invitations from many quarters to give lectures and talks. Young Christian workers were crying out for instruction and advice in the face of the unprecedented growth of Christianity throughout the country. In addition to his many weekly meetings and services at the Shanxi Road Church and his short-term Bible courses in the countryside, he gave advanced lectures on biblical studies at the Nanjing seminary and had deep discussions with the undergraduate students. His principle was "as long as there is a real demand I will come." He wrote articles in the journals of the seminary on preaching, and wrote books from his own deep experience of God: *The Way to God, God's Blessing in Sickness* and *St. John's Gospel.*

On Sunday, November 30, 1987 Pastor Fan Peiji preached to his large congregation in the Shanxi Road Church. His text was from 2 Corinthians 5:1: "For we know that when the tent that we live in on earth is folded up, there is a house built by God for us, an everlasting home not made by human hands, in the heavens" (JERUSALEM BIBLE). He preached with feeling and conviction on the temporary nature of our mortal lives and the certainty of an everlasting home prepared for us by God.

This was to be his last sermon, and how fitting it was. On Thursday, December 10, 1987 he was called home, having just attained the "three score years and ten" to which the psalmist refers. Since the day when he had stood up to dedicate his life to

Christ's service in the crowded meeting in Yantai in the days of his youth, he had given his all. The years interrupted by complex political events in his beloved country had only served to make him all the more determined to redeem the time and work harder when normality returned. For his widow, Yang Yunxiou, to whom he had been married forty-five years, his passing was a shock. She later wrote to me, telling of the deep peace the Lord gave her.

At the two crowded memorial services, organized by the church and his former art company, the response of his members and colleagues was one of determination to continue his work. Pastor Sheng Weiguang, chairman of the Ministry Committee of Shanxi Road Church, said that it was difficult to understand why God had taken Pastor Fan at that time of such great need in China, when the fast growing church so desperately needed teachers such as he. He expressed regret that a pastor of his standing had been given such poor housing and so low a wage, but this had not deterred him from giving his best. He said:

> Fan Peiji was our minister, and the footprints which he has left behind are beautiful. He has sown the seeds of truth in our hearts, and they will sprout and grow. We must walk in the footprints which he has left behind.

5

吴慕迦
WU MUJIA

1910–1997

The scholar who returned from prison to start all over again

> *When I fear my faith will fail,*
> *Christ can hold me fast.*
> *When the tempter would prevail,*
> *He can hold me fast.*
>
> *He will hold me fast,*
> *For my Saviour loves me so,*
> *He will hold me fast.*
> *—Ada R. Habershon*

Wu Mujia was born in 1910 in Tangshan, a town in northeast Hebei, which is now on the railway line running from Beijing to Beidaihe on the coast. To the north of Tangshan is the Great Wall which runs east and west in north China over mountains and valleys. Parts of it have fallen into decay or have entirely disappeared. The first stage of its construction took place in the third century B.C., when it was built to prevent attacks by the Tartars.

The province of Hebei suffers from dust storms, droughts and flooding; these natural disasters have caused much suffering to the local populace. Tangshan itself is subject to earthquakes, and in 1976 a quarter of a million people were killed in a large-scale disaster which devastated the whole area. A new Tangshan has arisen from the rubble.

Wu was born at a time of rapid political change in his motherland. After two and a half centuries, Manchu rule was waning. When he was a year old, fighting broke out between Imperial forces and revolutionaries who were determined to bring Manchu rule to an end. The Emperor abdicated, and in 1911 the Chinese Republic was proclaimed.

During Wu Mujia's childhood, Christian missions experienced great blessing. There was growth in church membership, in church buildings and in missionary institutions such as schools and hospitals. Wu Mujia was to benefit from these Christian activities.

His family was poor. His father constantly struggled to support his wife and children. Wu was a good student and did well in his studies, but from his earliest years he was aware that for him and his siblings to be able to attend school, his father had to borrow money. Throughout his childhood there was the constant burden of having to pay off debts.

When Wu Mujia finished his studies at middle school he was accepted as a student in a college of agriculture and forestry. He was uncertain as to what he really wanted to do in later life. He formed a close friendship with another boy at the college. One day this friend took him to a meeting which turned out to be a Christian one, without telling him in advance where they were going.

Wu was shocked to find himself in a Christian gathering— shocked that his friend could deceive him, and shocked at being involved in something he did not believe in. He wanted to walk out and return to the college, but he did not know the way. For the remainder of the service he was a captive worshipper. Not surprisingly he broke off his friendship.

At the age of nineteen he graduated from the college and became a teacher in Manchuria. Soon after Japan invaded and captured this area of China. It was to be the first crucial stage in the conquest of China. The new arrivals proclaimed the foundation of the "independent" state of Manchuria.

As a result of these political changes Wu lost his job as a teacher and returned to the family home in Tangshan, Hebei. He was unsettled and insecure. Life for his family was still a hand-to-mouth existence. He found that his father continued to struggle to support the family, and knew that he could not impose a further financial burden on him. Wu travelled around the area staying with friends and looking for secure employment. He tried the Army for a few months, and then did another stint of teaching in a middle school.

Wu was miserable and depressed. He could not find fulfilling and long-term work. His family was struggling on in poverty. His country was retreating before the disciplined soldiers of the Japanese Army, and in the skirmishes and raids the local people were suffering unspeakable hardships. In addition to these unfavourable circumstances his mind was full of questions about the purpose of life. How was the world created? What is the meaning of the universe? What is the purpose of life? He was bright and intelligent and could find no answers to these fundamental questions.

The young man had lost his way. He fell into bad company and evil habits. He did things that no one else knew about, but which he knew to be wrong. He recalls, "I knew that inside of me I was utterly corrupt. I had a sense of guilt about the things that I was doing. Life around me was unsettled. My country was being threatened by a powerful nation. I could not see any light, and my parents and my closest friends were unable to help me."

In the providence of God, things took an unexpected turn for the better. Wu moved to Henan province. One day he was waiting at a station for a train. A stranger on the platform said to him, "We have a long time to wait before the train comes. It is possible to attend a gospel service and still be back on time."

Wu agreed to go. At least this time he knew where he was going. He enjoyed the service. Afterwards he was invited to the home of a church worker who asked him to join her in a time of prayer. Hesitantly he agreed to do so. There on his knees he prayed aloud, "O God, I know that I am a sinner. Please forgive me for what I have done in the past. Please receive me as your child."

When he got up he felt a sense of peace in his heart and relief after the recent years of worry and uncertainty. He began reading the Bible, and experienced what the psalmist says, "How sweet are your words to my taste, sweeter than honey to my mouth!" (Psalm 119:103, NIV).

Soon after this he obtained permission to move permanently to the countryside of Henan, north of the Yellow River. He was keen to witness of his new-found faith in Christ. In his simple way he preached wherever he went, and taught the peasants to sing hymns and to learn some basic Bible verses. He grew steadily in his Christian faith and enjoyed sharing it with others.

Still unemployed, Wu lived very simply as he went from village to village preaching the gospel message. In one village he had an audience of about twenty adults, and his theme was "The great love of Jesus." As he preached he felt carried along by his message. The effect of this was that quite spontaneously he told his listeners that he wanted to spend the rest of his life preaching the gospel.

He had temporary accommodation at this time in a farmer's storeroom. In it was animal fodder and a rough bed. That was all he could afford. Wu says, "As soon as I announced that I wanted to serve God all my life as a preacher three letters arrived urging me to take a certain teaching post which had just fallen vacant. One of the writers was my former school headmaster."

It was just the kind of opening which the young man had previously been wanting. He knelt down in that rough storeroom and asked God for guidance. He became overwhelmed by a sense of God's power to cleanse people of their sins and give them

peace of heart. This was the message he was to preach. Bible verses
came to him with power and life, and with this came the conviction
that the message which he had been preaching in his faltering and
simple way was the message people needed.

In faith he declined the position offered him, and continued as a
travelling preacher. Wu later testified, "I have been serving God for
sixty years now. I have made mistakes, sometimes my faith has been
weak, but God has never left me. I know that when I turned down
that teaching post to serve God as a preacher I did the right thing."

In 1920, Dr. Watson Hayes, an American Presbyterian missionary, founded the Tengxian Theological Seminary in south
Shandong. It had grown to become one of the largest and most
influential seminaries in China. Wu heard good reports of it, and
was accepted as a student there in 1936. He studied there for
four years.

He recalls, "I achieved high marks in all my subjects. In my
third year I concentrated on English, Hebrew and Greek. Just
before I graduated I wrote a book for students on Hebrew."

At Tengxian seminary there was practical work to be done as
well as the academic studies. In his last two years, Wu took
services in the villages around Tengxian; this involved walking
long distances.

After graduation Wu Mujia became pastor of a Presbyterian
church in Beijing. It was at a time when the Chinese church was
emphasizing the importance of the "Three Self" principles of Self-
support, Self-government and Self-propagation. Chinese Christians
had relied too heavily on the funds of Western missions to pay for
their pastors' salaries and the maintenance of church buildings. The
missionaries had led in the running of the churches and been slow
to delegate responsibility to Chinese Christians. Chinese had been
all too quick to allow the missionaries to plan evangelistic outreach
and extension. "He who pays the piper calls the tune."

Young pastors were told that they must shoulder greater responsibility and encourage their church members to give in such a way that self-support could be achieved. Wu was confident that he could lead his church into carrying out the Three Self principles. It was an extremely busy time for him. Pastor Wu had to prepare sermons for every week of the year, and to put into practice the expository preaching which he had been taught at Tengxian.

Sudden changes came when Japanese planes attacked the American Navy in Pearl Harbor. The Japanese were already in occupation around him in north China, but now the war was extended to involve other nations, who up to now had been recognized as neutrals. Britain and America were now, as far as Japan was concerned, enemy nations. In March 1943 all of Wu's missionary colleagues were sent into internment in a camp in Weixian, Shandong.

The churches in Beijing had been trying to prepare themselves for the day when the missionary societies would have to withdraw, but Wu soon realized that, following the departure of missionaries to Weixian and the changing economic situation, finances were steadily decreasing. There were now insufficient funds for his salary. Wu Mujia examined himself. Had he not put his very best into his pastoral and preaching work?

Whenever there were doubts or discouragement a verse from a hymn and a verse from the Bible would come to him. He had been taught them in the early days of his Christian life:

> *When I fear my faith will fail,*
> *Christ can hold me fast.*
> *When the tempter would prevail,*
> *He can hold me fast.*
>
> *He will hold me fast,*
> *For my Saviour loves me so,*
> *He will hold me fast.*

One of the verses in the Bible that meant much to him in these days came from the mouth of Jesus: "I give unto them eternal life; and they shall never perish, neither shall any *man* pluck them out of my hand" (John 10:28, KJV). These words assured him that the powerful hands of Jesus would always hold him firmly.

Perhaps God wanted him to stop his busy schedule in order to learn some valuable lessons. He joined an informal group in Xiangshan, not far from Beijing's Summer Palace. In these beautiful surroundings and under regular faithful preaching he continued to examine his life. He realized that he had a cool and calculating mind, and lacked a warm and loving heart towards other people.

In this unstructured group of Christians, Wu's spiritual life began to flower. He warmed to the leader and his happy family. In spite of physical weaknesses this preacher spoke with power and relevance. Whenever it came to Wu Mujia's turn to lead the devotions he found that, in this quiet environment which had enabled him to wait upon God, his messages came clearly and unmistakably to his mind, and were delivered with spiritual freedom and power.

During the last four years of the Sino-Japanese War, Wu and his family had been "living by faith." This involved not telling anyone of their needs, and praying together for these needs to be provided. His wife, Xu Xingwu, had joined fully in this lifestyle of depending daily on God's provision.

Living at Xiangshan also gave Wu time for careful Bible study. In fact he read right through the Old Testament in the original Hebrew. As he went out on Sundays to preach in different churches in and around Beijing he was conscious of greater spiritual power in his ministry. His preaching brought a response. He reminded himself that to continue to have God's blessing on his ministry he must keep humble before him, and avoid having spiritual pride and self confidence.

The end of the war with Japan in 1945 did not bring peace to China, for the civil war between the KMT and the Communists only intensified. Thousands of university students who had fled to west China from the bombings in northeast China were now returning to their homes, and this created a great opportunity for Christian witness among these young people. Wu now divided his time between serving a Beijing church and working for the Inter-Varsity Fellowship among students.

Upon their return to the northeast the students were disappointed. They had entertained hopes of completing their studies, which had been disrupted by war, in peaceful surroundings. But they soon became aware of the presence of Communist guerrillas in and around Beijing, as well as of Communist cells in every college. Also, the students were distressed at the failure of the KMT government to keep back the Communist advance, to halt soaring inflation and to give them adequate grants for their living conditions. Student demonstrations could be seen on the streets with young people carrying banners on which were slogans such as "End the civil war" and "End our empty stomachs." Some of these incidents ended in bloodshed.

At this critical juncture a remarkable spiritual movement was developing among the university students. In nearly every institution of higher learning, groups were meeting together for Bible study and prayer, and their numbers were rapidly growing. Leslie Lyall of the China Inland Mission arrived in Beijing in 1946 and was providentially given a spacious rented house; this was to become the centre of a hive of student activity for the following two years.

The property included a spacious hall that could seat 200 people. At 8 a.m. every Sunday there was a service for students. Conferences were also held at an orphanage near the Summer Palace. The students were bursting with spiritual life and enthusiasm. As they were driven back to their campuses they sang hymns of praise to God loudly and boldly.

Pastor Wu worked closely with Leslie Lyall in running these meetings. It was a high point in his Christian ministry, for there were many conversions and acts of reconsecration. He enjoyed expounding the Scriptures to these eager students. The numbers continued to grow and students had to be packed tightly into the meeting rooms.

Wu and his family stayed with the Lyall family for three months during 1948, praying with them and discussing with them what Christians should do in a future Communist government. Before the end of the year the Lyalls returned to Shanghai with the student revival still in progress.

Wu was becoming increasingly aware of radical changes taking place politically. The Communists were gaining control of an increasing number of towns and cities in China. Christians had traditionally supported the government of Chiang Kaishek, but it was now clear that he had lost control of the country's affairs. He had failed to address the desperate needs of the peasants in their poverty and exploitation. Although there was corruption and inefficiency in his government, Christians realized there was freedom to worship and evangelize under Chiang. There was widespread fear that a new government would be bitterly opposed to Christianity.

Wu was reminded of a verse in the Book of Acts which said, "...we must through much tribulation enter into the kingdom of God" (Acts 14:22, KJV). He would also remind himself of that hymn which said, "He will hold me fast." Storm clouds were gathering on the horizon, but God would not leave him. Wu told his colleagues, "There is clearly trouble ahead of us and we are going to suffer as Christians, but the church in China will survive these trials."

At the well-attended student conferences held at this time the speakers were Wang Mingdao and Calvin Chao, and their emphasis was on preparing for suffering. Many of those who listened would within a decade be undergoing a severe trial of their faith. In the informal discussions it was clear that the students had no desire to collaborate with any future Communist government in any shape or form.

It was in October 1949 that Mao Zedong declared the establishment of the People's Republic of China with the now famous words, "We have stood up." Over the months and years that followed these momentous words there was increasing control over Christian activities. When not preaching on Sundays Wu attended the services at the Tabernacle where Wang Mingdao was preaching fearlessly. He had regular times of discussion and prayer with Wang. What should they do in response to the demands for total loyalty made by the new rulers? Wang's reaction was unequivocal. We cannot compromise the Lordship of Christ over his church.

In 1950 the *Christian Manifesto* issued by church leaders who were co-operating with the new rulers made it clear that for Christians in China the road ahead would be even harder than anticipated. This document showed that the Communist authorities would be demanding a high price for even a semblance of religious liberty. By the end of 1951 all but a few foreign missionaries had left the country.

The new regime certainly brought stability, freedom from external debts, as well as land redistribution and reclamation. It eliminated banditry, concubinage and corruption, and introduced health care, large-scale education and neighbourhood committees. But the other side of the coin was that it proved to be a totalitarian and coercive regime that subjected those who deviated from its regulations to imprisonment or banishment to distant parts of the country. "Accusation Meetings" were held in the main centres all over the country and Beijing was bound to have its turn.

As Wu went about his work among students, he kept singing to himself, "He will hold me fast." He was aware of his weakness and frailty, and prayed to be kept faithful in the hour of trial, whenever it might come.

In 1954 his friend Wang Mingdao was brought before a public Accusation meeting, at which some in the crowd even demanded the death penalty, while the majority present remained strangely silent. The Christian students in the city, who had sat under Wang's preaching, both at the Tabernacle and in the student conferences, mounted a vigorous opposition to these public trials.

They marched through the main streets carrying banners with slogans that said, "Oppose the persecution of Wang Mingdao." Their bold actions drew favourable responses from far beyond the confines of the Christian community, for support for their cause spread throughout Beijing, as well as to other parts of China.

Next it was Wu Mujia's turn. He was arrested and faced a trial as a result of which he was classified as a dangerous counter-revolutionary. He was alleged to be the "black hand" behind the activities of the local Christian students, and to have manipulated their negative response to the new government. His primary accuser was a churchman who had been the leader of the smaller Student Christian Movement group of students. It is interesting to note that about thirty years later when this churchman had an opportunity to attend a conference abroad he returned with a valuable Bible commentary which he gave to Wu, to express his regret at what he had done.

Wang was finally arrested on August 8, 1955, and Wu's arrest followed 20 days later on August 28. Wu found that he was in the cell next to Wang. His guards told him that they wanted him to hear what was happening to Wang, as a warning as to what might happen to him. Wu prayed for Wang's well-being, and could only sing under his breath to himself, "He will hold me fast."

Wang was given a life sentence and was sent to a prison in Taiyuan, Shanxi province. Soon afterwards Wu Mujia was given a similar sentence and sent to the same province, and then later to Manchuria.

Before departing Wu had the heart-breaking task of saying good-bye to his family and friends. He had to part with his dear wife and small children, who would now have no breadwinner to support them. At the time when he left home his family only had half a yuan! They had been living by faith off and on for many years, and so had already learned to trust their faithful heavenly Father.

As Wu was taken away from Beijing by guards he found comfort in two things. First, he had two younger sisters who were in regular employment and who would be able to support his aged parents. Second, his wife Xingwu was already a mature woman of faith. She would continue to bring up the children in the Christian faith, though it would have to be done discreetly.

The next chapter of his life would be a long and trying one—twenty-three years of loneliness, hardship and testing. Far from home, he had no family to love, no Bible to read, no fellowship with other Christians. After a time he was stopped even from praying, though he continued to do so surreptitiously. The Psalmist says:

> *If* I take the wings of the morning,
> And dwell in the uttermost parts of the sea,
> Even there Your hand shall lead me,
> And Your right hand shall hold me
> (Psalm 139:9–10, NKJV).

For long hours each day Wu worked as a labourer in the fields, growing vegetables. In his spare time he was given approved books to read on Marxism and Leninism, Chinese History and Chinese Literature. He read and studied the poetry of the Tang and Song dynasties, especially those of Li Bai, Du Fu and Xing Jiaxian. He tried to memorize many of the verses. Twelve centuries previously Li Bai (A.D. 701–762) had written:

> *The moon shines brightly on my bed.*
> *It looks like frost on the floor.*
> *I looked up at the bright moon,*
> *And looked down, missing my hometown.*

He thought of his loved ones in faraway Beijing. Looking back on this time in prison, Wu Mujia says:

> During this long period I was spiritually weak and made many mistakes. I keenly missed having no family, no Bible

and no Christian fellowship. Doubts came to me from time to time, and I seriously considered giving up my faith.

One summer's evening I was working alone in a vegetable field. Above me the sky was clear and the stars were shining. All around me was quiet. While I was working I was alone with my thoughts.

There in the field he pondered the doubts that had been flooding his mind, and he came to a firm conclusion which settled it for him once and for all:

I could not deny the experiences that I had had of forgiveness by my Saviour and his power in my life. I could not deny that God had often heard my prayers, and that the Holy Spirit had guided me.

Wu resolved that he could not abandon his faith. God had done so much for him. The only thing which caused him concern was that the years of his life were speeding by and he would soon be an old man. But he knew that his times were in God's hands.

The few letters which reached him from his wife showed that her faith was still strong and her morale high. Their heavenly Father was supplying the family's every need. Week after week a knock at the door of their home would draw Mrs. Wu to the door to find a bag of potatoes or flour or vegetables, and articles of clothing for the children. Hearts had been touched to feed this needy family.

Then his dear wife Xingwu fell ill with an advanced condition of lung cancer, and she went slowly downhill. In her weakness she pleaded with the authorities to allow her to see her husband before dying. But this was refused. Was he not a dangerous counter-revolutionary? As she slipped away with her two daughters at her bedside she whispered feebly words of love to "Mujia."

One day, the years of reform-through-labour imprisonment came to an end. Following the death of Chairman Mao in 1976 China had turned a corner, and the era of revolution and violent struggle was followed by an era of reform and consolidation. Among Deng Xiaoping's many reforms was the release of political prisoners in 1978–1979. All who were over sixty years of age and had been imprisoned for more than twenty years could be released.

Whilst it was good to be a free man and able to return to Beijing for Wu Mujia it was not an easy process. He told me that for him the most painful part of his return was the absence of his beloved wife. He showed me a small framed photo of her that he had kept all through his imprisonment. When he was staying with Leslie Lyall the missionary had given him a box camera, and with it he had taken a photo of Xingwu. "That," he told me, "is all I have from the past."

Wu's children had grown up and left home. His books and other belongings were all gone. The government allocated him an apartment in northwest Beijing. At seventy, he was starting life all over again, having spent more than a third of it in prison. But as he told me his story there was no trace of bitterness about the past, only a recognition of God's goodness to him.

When asked by a Methodist minister from Britain what he had learned during his imprisonment, Wu gave a thoughtful and moving reply:

> I discovered my own weakness and my need of the Lord. I learned that God is wonderfully gracious. I came to know his love, and now see that he was preparing me to take hold of the present opportunities to serve him. Why, during the Cultural Revolution, when the Church was being severely persecuted and some Christians died, I was kept safe in prison! God kept me safe so that I can serve him today.[1]

A young Beijing pastor described to me the new vigour with which Wu began to plan his future. "He was determined to spend

---

[1] Geoffrey R. Senior, *For Love of the Chinese* (Plymouth: E.J. Rickard Ltd, 1989), 118.

Wu Mujia spent twenty-three years in a forced labour camp before being released at the age of seventy. He went on to teach Greek and Hebrew at Yanjing Seminary.

the remaining years of his life expending his energies and skills for the Lord. He wanted to make up for lost time, and he renewed his commitment to serve God for his remaining years."

But what was he to do? He spent long periods in prayer, asking God for guidance. A message came from the principal of the local Yanjing Seminary, Pastor Ying Jizeng, a friend from Tengxian seminary days, inviting him to teach Greek and Hebrew there. Was this the answer for which he had been praying? As he prayed about it he told the Lord, "But they took a different stand to me in the Accusation Meetings." The Lord seemed to be saying, "That is all in the past." Then he asked the Lord for a sign to make his will absolutely clear. "If I am to teach at the seminary I will need a *Thayer's Greek/English Lexicon*. If you supply me with one I will know unmistakably that this is your will."

The following day there was a knock at the door and a friend, Pastor Wang Zhen, came into his apartment with the lexicon for which he had been praying. For fifteen years Wu taught at the seminary and found rich fulfillment in it. During this period he also wrote a number of commentaries in Chinese on various books of the New Testament. These have been widely used by pastors in China.

The story of Wu Mujia illustrates the fact that some leading Chinese Christians, having vigorously opposed the Communist regime at the time of Liberation on the grounds that it was demanding the total allegiance of its citizens, revised their strategy in later years when Deng Xiaoping granted a greater degree of freedom and flexibility to the churches. Consequently many godly pastors today are working within the restraints of the Religious Affairs Bureau (RAB) and the Three Self Patriotic Movement (TSPM), believing that their ministry can have a wider influence within these structures as against staying outside. Other equally godly preachers remain convinced that to work within the TSPM is to undermine the Lordship of Christ over the local church. Possibly as many as two thirds of China's Christians worship in house churches for this reason at considerable risk of arrest and imprisonment.

As a result of his decision to serve God in the RAB-controlled Yanjing seminary teaching Hebrew and Greek to successive classes of theological students, Wu has undoubtedly exercised a wide spiritual influence. He has also preached in the large Chong Wen Men church in central Beijing. From this it will be seen that his early strictures on the Communist government have been considerably modified. Others who were imprisoned in the same period as Wu returned, on being released, to their home cities to continue advocating non-co-operation with the TSPM.

On my visits to China I have found my way to Wu Mujia's modest apartment in northwest Beijing. One evening, after a sumptuous Chinese meal, he recounted to me his harsh experiences of earlier years. But in looking back he was always very positive that the hand of God was in it all, and there was no trace of bitterness towards those who had betrayed him or caused him to be banished far from his loved ones. Wu now saw God's hand in his imprisonment. While other pastors were suffering during the Cultural Revolution, marched through the streets wearing dunce caps and carrying heavy slogans which said "running dogs of the imperialists," he was safe in his prison in northeastern China, preserved for serving God in future happier years. That was his way of looking at it.

In a testimony that Wu Mujia wrote towards the end of his life he quoted the words of David: "Surely goodness and mercy shall follow me all the days of my life: and I will dwell in the house of the Lord for ever" (Psalm 23:6, KJV).

He died on March 26, 1997 at the age of eighty-seven. The hymn which he had frequently sung to himself to assure himself of God's love had proven true:

> *He will hold me fast.*
> *For my Saviour loves me so*
> *He will hold me fast.*

6

吳光亞
GRAHAM WU
(WU GUANGYA)

Medical missionary to the Miao people and bold lay preacher

On October 14, 1940 Wu Guangya, aged 16, wrote on a piece of paper, "Today I want to make a promise to Jesus to serve him for ever and to strive to do his will." Half a century later he commented, "I have tried to keep that promise, though sometimes I have been weak, but God has always stood by me."

Wu Guangya was born in 1924 in Iyang in the picturesque and mountainous province of Hunan. Three years earlier the Chinese Communist Party had been formed in Shanghai by two men. One was the librarian of Beijing University and the other his young assistant from Hunan, Mao Zedong. Mao came from humble beginnings, for his father owned a small patch of land in Shaoshan, southwest of Changsha, on which he grew rice. Hunan has produced many of China's political leaders.

Historically this province was always resistant to change. It displayed an antipathy to all things foreign. At the beginning of the twentieth century, when the nation was adopting Western education and technology, this province, deep in central China, stubbornly resisted such changes. And in 1890, when the early bearers of the gospel came to Hunan, the people of Changsha issued anti-Christian tracts, which they dispatched far and wide.

Hunan was the last province in China to allow missionaries to enter and reside. My great-grandmother, Amelia Broomhall, working at the CIM headquarters in London, had a special place in her prayers for this province. In the "Obituary" to her in *China's Millions* Mrs. Howard Taylor said of her that "she laid hold on God for the intensely anti-foreign province of Hunan." It is remarkable that Hudson Taylor died while on a brief visit to Changsha in 1905, and was received with affection and esteem by the local Chinese church leaders. His biographer, Dr. A.J. Broomhall comments, "For Hudson Taylor to stand on Hunan soil and set foot on CIM premises there marked in a sense the crowning moment of his life." It was a fitting finale to the life of a man who often said, "If I had a thousand lives I would give them all to China."[1]

As we shall see, Wu Guangya's spiritual life was moulded on the spiritual principles of Hudson Taylor. He read and re-read in its original English the thick two-volumed life of this pioneer missionary to China written by Dr. and Mrs. Howard Taylor. Wu has often stated, "Next to the Bible, Hudson Taylor's biography has helped me most to understand God."

Wu's father, Wu Sezhu, had been a peasant farmer in Pingjiang, northeast of Changsha. He worked in a beautiful countryside of plains, valleys and well-wooded hills. As he laboured in the terraced rice fields he could look across to ranges of mountains with fertile valleys between them. In 1912 the British Methodists commenced work in this county. John Stanfield later referred to Pingjiang as one of the most flourishing of all the Methodist circuits. Soon after the

---

[1] On the life and ministry of Hudson Taylor (1832–1905), see A.J. Broomhall, "It is not death to die!" in *Hudson Taylor & China's Open Century*, vol. 7 (London: Hodder & Stoughton, 1989), 507.

missionaries arrived Wu Sezhu heard some Chinese evangelists preaching the gospel. It seemed that Wu's heart had been prepared for their message, for he resolved to follow the Jesus way. He attended Bible studies, eager to hear all he could about the Christian faith.

The local Chinese pastor, seeing the farmer's deep interest and fervour, suggested that he go for theological training at the nearby seminary in Wuchang in order to become a preacher. The farmer replied that he did not want to relinquish his business, and so the pastor told him the parable of the rich fool, in which God asked the man who had accumulated much of this world's wealth, "Who is going to possess all that you have prepared?" (Luke 12:20, J.B. PHILLIPS). This argument convinced Wu Sezhu, who decided to spend the rest of his life serving the Lord. He changed his name from "becoming rich" to "serving the Lord" (pronounced the same but using different Chinese characters), went to seminary and worked as a pastor in the Methodist Church for thirty years, retiring in 1942.

Thus Wu Guangya was a "son of the manse." He heard about Jesus Christ from his earliest years. When he was six years old it was time to go to school, but there was rioting and political unrest in the neighbourhood, and so his father suggested that he learn his elementary lessons at home. When he was awakened each morning his father would ask him to write down some new character which he had learned, or to explain a passage from the Bible. After two years he had covered the whole of the New Testament.

From his earliest years Guangya wanted to serve God, and his father gave him every encouragement. At church on Sundays, his father would call him to the front to recite some verses from the Bible or sing a hymn. In this way public speaking came naturally to the young boy.

When the school boy was eight years old he was enrolled in the Methodist boarding school at Pingjiang. He was quick to learn his lessons, but was often hungry, for his father gave him less pocket money than the other students received. Then he sat entry exams for the secondary school, and was in the top four. Here the food was better and he was able to study without feeling weak with hunger. It was while he was here that Guangya had the first of three brushes with death which he was to experience in his youth, each one serving to remind him that God was protecting him for future service. He was swimming in the Liuyang River and was beginning to be carried away by the strong current. Providentially a small boat came by and he was rescued.

As high school days approached he applied for a scholarship from the Methodist Church. Two were awarded each year to the best students, and Guangya won one of them. At the beginning of the century three men had gone out from Yale University and founded a "Yale-in-China" project (called in Chinese *Xiang Ya*), which began in Changsha. In co-operation with the Hunan provincial government they built a magnificent hospital, college, high school, nursing school and a medical training centre.

It was to the Yale-in-China high school that the young student went. Upon arrival he was impressed with its classrooms, science laboratories, sports ground and swimming pool. But after only one day Changsha began to suffer devastating air raids from the Japanese. To add to this the Chinese military personnel ordered the destruction of the city to prevent it falling into the hands of the enemy. In the bombing and destruction of Changsha many of the inhabitants were killed. Though bombs fell around him, Guangya was unharmed.

Thus the school had to evacuate to inferior premises in Yuanling, which was near the mountain range overlooking the River Yuan. The Yale-in-China high school was a good one, both academically and spiritually. Here the young student received Christian teaching from lecturers who were themselves committed Christians. It was here, at the age of fifteen, that Guangya faced death once again. He was a strong swimmer, but while swimming one day in a river the strong current swept him out into the middle of the stream. Mr. Gulick, an American teacher, saw that the student was in danger of drowning and acted quickly. He asked the other students to take off their belts and tie them together in a long chain. With this Wu was brought back to the shore and to safety. God had plans for him in future years.

It was at this time that the American staff gave him the English name of Graham. This is a name that he uses to this day.

When Wu was sixteen years old he had an experience of God that changed his life. On October 14, 1940 he wrote on a piece of paper:

> Today I want to make a promise to Jesus to serve him for ever and to strive to do his will.

Looking back to that decision half a century later Wu comments, "I have tried to keep that promise, though sometimes I have been weak, but God has always stood by me."

To his family and friends Wu always appeared to be a model and upright young person. He had refrained from the drinking and smoking in which some of his classmates indulged. He had never been heard to swear or say unkind things. He had read the Bible and prayed regularly. But the person that they saw was really quite different. He had done many wrong things, but had been clever and subtle about it.

With careful planning he had stolen sweets and biscuits from his mother. Before doing this he would close all the doors but never lock them, whilst his brother had locked the doors in order to steal, and thus been challenged and caught. Wu had also stolen small amounts of money from his parents and lied about his actions.

With his conversion came the overwhelming desire to make restitution and confession of his past wrongdoings, and to pay back the things that he had stolen. He had taken a school volleyball, and so he bought a new one, returned it to the school, and publicly confessed what he had done. He confessed his past mistakes to the Christian fellowship at the high school, even though he feared that he would lose his position as its chairman. From that day to this Wu has kept "short accounts with God," putting the smallest things right as soon as he was convicted of their wrongness.

With the end of his high school days approaching Wu began to consider what further studies he should pursue. He was drawn to medicine, and in good Chinese tradition asked his father for approval. Pastor Wu had hoped that he would either become a pastor or a teacher, but he willingly gave his approval.

He then applied for a scholarship to study at Xiang Ya (Yale-in-China) medical college, and passed his entry exams. The Japanese air raids and fighting had uprooted the normal life of many Chinese universities. Students and whole university groups fled the war zones and moved under dangerous conditions to the provinces of Sichuan, Guizhou and Yunnan. Thus the Xiang Ya medical college moved from Changsha to Guiyang in Guizhou. At the beginning of the medical course the students had to study Chinese Politics and English. Graham Wu mastered these subjects, but of the sixty who commenced with him only thirty entered the second year's studies.

It was while studying here in 1941 that the college student had his third brush with death. There had been some crowded Double Tenth (October 10) celebrations, attended by hundreds of people from the town. A fire was caused by some firecrackers, and flames threatened the safety of the building in which they were sitting. Wu joined the panicking crowds rushing for the doors, but in the panic he fell to the floor and lost his shoes. One person was killed in the crush, but Wu was assisted to the door and to fresh air. He sang a hymn of praise to God for his deliverance.

The Japanese advance eventually reached Guiyang in 1942, and life became difficult for the inhabitants of the city. Wu was working on a shoe-string budget and regularly asked God to help him through his studies. It was at this time that the college student read the two copious volumes of Hudson Taylor's life, *The Growth of a Soul* and *The Growth of a Work for God*. For him this was a life-changing and life-challenging experience. From this time on he built his spiritual life on the spiritual principles of this godly missionary to China. He was deeply moved as he read of Hudson Taylor's physical needs being met and of the problems that he encountered in his pioneer work, problems which were overcome through prayer and faith. This encouraged him to trust the Lord for all his needs and in all his difficulties.

In 1945 the ravages of war forced the refugee medical college to make a second move away from the fighting. The entire unit moved on to Chongqing. But the problem was that with the air raids and bombings everyone else was also on the move. Transport was at a premium. Wu's sister and brother-in-law were also in Guiyang, and likewise needed to move to Chongqing from the war zone.

Wu Guangya found a verse from the Psalms at this time that gave him assurance and peace of mind about the move:

> For the oppression of the poor, for the sighing of the needy, now will I arise, saith the Lord; I will set *him* in safety *from him* that puffeth at him (Psalm 12:5, KJV).

He confidently told his sister, "God has told me not to worry about transport to Chongqing." Although she was a Christian she ignored him, but the following day Wu's brother-in-law found a vehicle going to Chongqing. Into it piled Wu, his sister and brother-in-law and some close friends, and their basic belongings. They found suitable accommodation upon arrival, and Wu was able to continue his studies.

At the re-organized medical college in Chongqing Wu was elected Chairman of the "Students' Freedom Society," a position which he had neither sought nor wanted. This appointment placed the student in an awkward position. He was wary of the influence of

Marxism on the campus, and he was expected to fall in line with the new ideas that were sweeping through the college. He knew that it would involve co-operating with the college authorities, though his convictions as a Christian were at variance with theirs. If he were to speak out against the new programme there would be a rumpus on the campus. What was he to do?

He thought and prayed about the matter, and an idea came to him. He told a fellow Christian student about his dilemma and asked him to find an excuse to fire him. His friend complied and the problem was resolved.

———

Now let me tell you the story of Wu Guangya's romance. Back in 1942 while in his second year of studies at the Xiang Ya medical college he met Miss Zhou Yaozhen, a first-year student. They met through the meetings of the college Christian fellowship. Wu fell in love with the young student and soon it was mutual. Love blossomed into romance.

Soon, however, Zhou fell ill with meningitis and was hospitalized a few miles from the medical college. As a result, she fell behind in her studies. Zhou had been orphaned at the age of five and had few relatives or friends. Graham, however, was a regular visitor to the hospital and their friendship continued to grow. Sadly, with the escalation of the Japanese War, Graham had to move to Guiyang and then Chongqing. The two young people kept in touch by frequent letters.

As the day of his graduation drew nearer, Graham Wu had to consider his future. He was approached about working in a small "Yale-in-Miao" hospital in Yuanling in northwestern Hunan. This hospital/clinic was an extension of the Yale-in-China hospital based in Changsha. There was already an experienced doctor there leading the work, but he was desperately short-staffed. Would Wu consider going to the Yuanling hospital?

A struggle went on in Wu Guangya's heart. From a material

point of view there was little in this proposal to attract him. The area was poor, the working hours were long and the salary exceptionally low. His fellow graduates would be proceeding to responsible posts in large hospitals, with the prospect of further advancement, and here he was being asked to work in a remote hospital under conditions that were far from attractive.

Wu fasted and prayed about it. Sometimes his mind and heart resisted the proposed move; other times he was quite willing to respond to the challenge. Eventually the spiritual battle was won, and he advised the trustees that he would go. He came to view it as a missionary opportunity. During the day he would care for their bodies, and in the evenings care for their souls.

The Wulingyuan area to which Wu was going was home to three of Hunan's minority peoples—the Tujia, the Miao and the Bai nationalities. Wu would live among the Miao tribe. Larger groupings of this tribe inhabited parts of Yunnan and Guizhou provinces. The Chinese despised and marginalized these aboriginal tribes in the southwest; their forebears had pushed these tribes westward to the less fertile hinterland. The KMT government was now taking more progressive action to improve their welfare.

Like his role model Hudson Taylor, Wu Guangya, now a qualified doctor, took a bold step of faith and went to serve a tribe of a different culture in an isolated region of China. He applied himself conscientiously to the work in this needy area. It was gratifying to know that his skills were needed, and that there was a spiritual opportunity here.

Two months after his arrival Dr. Wang, the head of the hospital, arranged to have a much-needed holiday, since he had not had a break for ten years. Wu, the new and inexperienced doctor, asked himself how he could cope as doctor in charge. He made it a matter of prayer and made two requests to God: (1) to give him the skill and judgment to make the right decisions; and (2) not to send to the hospital patients needing treatment which he was unable to give. His prayers were answered, for everything went smoothly during Dr. Wang's absence.

In 1947 Dr. Wu took three helpers with him to open a new clinic in Jishou to the west of Yuanling. They occupied a small church building—the doctor, assistants and patients all crowded into the same house. He had been hesitant about moving from a small country hospital to a new clinic where there would be no surgery, only a pharmacy. Again he thought of his classmates who would be moving to larger hospitals and to more prestigious posts. Then he reminded himself of Hudson Taylor and the difficulties the early CIM missionaries had experienced in inland China. Their problems must have been far greater than his, he reflected.

Again the clinic was in a Miao area, and there were about 4,000 inhabitants. The medical team's chief weapon for battling the many infectious diseases among the poor was penicillin. An alarm clock would ring every three hours to ensure that penicillin injections were given by the team to the patients.

By 1947 the Japanese War had been over for two years. Wu returned to Changsha where reconstruction was going on to repair the ravages of war. Zhou was now out of hospital and had resumed her medical studies. The young man approached the young lady and proposed marriage to her, pressing her to help in the work that he would be doing in Yuanling.

"The course of true love never did run smooth." Although Zhou loved Wu deeply, she lacked self confidence, and did not see herself as a suitable wife for the newly qualified doctor. She said that she would help in the work at the small hospital, but could not marry him. Her reasons for not wanting to marry were four-fold: (1) she was two years older than Wu—this was an unsuitable age gap; (2) she had serious health problems; (3) having been orphaned she had had no experience of family life; and (4) she was not suited to looking after children. Wu, the earnest suitor, eliminated Zhou's objections one by one, and they were engaged to be married. Following traditional Chinese etiquette, Wu obtained the agreement and approval of both families.

———

The workload at Jishou increased. Although Wu had taken on more assistants, they were neither well-educated nor qualified. So he wrote to Zhou to come and help. She was now in her fourth year of medical studies and would have to stop her course to come and help. Not having completed her studies she would have to come as an unqualified medical worker. This meant that she would not be qualified to perform operations, though there was plenty of other work which she could do. Zhou prayed about this with another friend at university, and finally felt clearly guided to proceed with the marriage and join Wu in his important work.

Dr. Wu went to Hankou for the wedding. On the morning of the wedding he noticed that his bride was not looking happy. He read to her some words from the book of Jeremiah:

> "I have loved you with an everlasting love; I have drawn you with loving-kindness"(Jeremiah 31:3, NIV).

Zhou responded and brightened up. They were married by a Chinese pastor on April 26, 1948. In good Chinese tradition they travelled on a sedan chair. It was a marriage that was to be blessed by God. They have recently celebrated their golden wedding anniversary. The marriage has been blessed with a son and two daughters.

———

Wu was eager to be of service to the local community in every possible way. There was, for example, the incident when a girl of twelve jumped into the river near the hospital to commit suicide.

Her father had a mental problem and she had had such a bitter argument with her mother about him that the girl decided to end her life. Wu jumped into the river and brought her back to the shore. He asked her mother if she could stay with the medical team at the small hospital and assist in the work; she agreed. The girl became a useful member of the family of workers and eventually became the matron. She professed faith in Christ, though she reneged after the victory of the Communists.

It was good to have Mrs. Wu helping in the medical work. The clinic expanded steadily and more buildings had to be purchased and additional equipment obtained. There were now facilities for 28 patients, as well as many more outpatients. The hospital now had special departments for specific needs—for surgery, maternity, geriatrics and so on. Word soon got around that loving and efficient service was rendered at the hospital, and the Miao people came along in increasing numbers. These simple peasant people showed their gratitude in many ways for the loving care they received.

The medical staff now consisted of fourteen workers. They were a large happy family, living under the same roof. Their wages were a mere pittance, but the job satisfaction made up for that. Both staff and patients ate the same simple food. Dr. and Mrs. Wu were happy in the work, knowing that they were doing God's will.

Graham Wu, however, was fully aware of the political unrest around him. Everywhere there was dissatisfaction with the incompetence of the KMT. It was clear that a Communist government would soon be in power and would bring radical changes to the social and political structure of the country. He lived one day at a time, and prayed for guidance as to how he should respond to the inevitable changes.

In September 1949 Yuanling was liberated, but strangely the hospital was still KMT-controlled. Initially Wu could travel freely between liberated and non-liberated areas as a doctor. When the

Communists had full control of the area they changed the name of the hospital from Great Grace Hospital to New Life Hospital. As a matter of principle the hospital continued to serve anyone needing medical attention, whether KMT or Communist.

Wu was a man of precision, with a strong sense of right and wrong regarding the smallest detail. He decided from the first day of Liberation to adhere to his Christian principles. He refused to join in the shouting or singing of "Long live Chairman Mao." "No one can expect to live for ten thousand years," Wu asserted. He could only conscientiously exclaim, "Good health to Chairman Mao." During the public campaign "Resist America and Aid Korea" he firmly refused to contribute funds to the Korean War, asserting that as a Christian he could not help to buy weapons; he could only give money for medical work. He was publicly asked to state which country was good, South Korea or North Korea. He replied, "From the newspaper reports North Korea is better, but the Bible says that everyone has sinned, no one is right." But there were aspects of Mao's programme with which Wu was in full agreement, such as the provision of education and health services to all, and the sending out of the urban population into the country to help grow more food.

In September 1952 Mr. She, governor of the county, having heard of Wu's refusal to conform, warned him that his job could be in jeopardy if he continued to practise his religious faith. He pressed the doctor by saying, "All you need to do is to publicly renounce your faith." But Wu firmly refused. Mr. She then said ominously to Graham Wu, "You will hear more about this within the next twenty years." Four years later he would be put in prison.

The changes, inevitable under the new regime, now began. Dr. Wang had retired from the work at Yuanling hospital, and Dr. Wu was appointed to take his place. This involved serving on the Chinese People's Political Consultative Committee, and he knew that this would create a very delicate situation for him as a Christian. On the one hand his very position as head doctor put him in a position of authority and public respect, but on the other hand situations were bound to arise where his loyalty to Christ would be at stake.

After Liberation Dr. Wu's wife, Zhou Yaozhen, had returned to Changsha to complete her medical studies. When she qualified Wu wrote to Mr. Li Dequan, the Minister of Public Health in Beijing, to allow her to return to Jishou. This was granted, and Wu comments in his diary that he always found the central government more reasonable than the provincial government, which was disapproving of his stand as a Christian.

Close on the heels of the "Resist America and Aid Korea" drive came the Three Antis and Five Antis campaigns[2] in 1949, all designed to eliminate counter-revolutionaries. Wu knew that he was regarded as belonging to this category of people. When he was given promotion and instructed to move to a new position in the Bureau of Public Health in Changsha he was pleased, for it released him from the precarious position which he was holding as the senior doctor of a hospital. Knowing that the Five Antis campaign could be directed at him, he asked his superiors whether he should proceed to Changsha before the campaign or after. He was told to go immediately.

His new position was Director of a Health Workers Association. This was a pleasant change after the pressures of the hospital work and the demands that had been made on him by government officials. It involved standing up for the rights of the health workers, listening to their complaints and setting up sanitoriums for rest and recuperation. It also involved considerable travel and consultation with officials in other places. On one of his journeys to Beijing, Wu stayed with Wang Mingdao for three days. He had a great respect and admiration for this famous preacher, and had long talks with him about the situation then prevailing in China.

---

[2] The Three Antis were corruption, waste and bureaucracy. The Five Antis were bribery, smuggling, stealing national resources, skimping on work and materials and stealing national economic reports.

Wang was bitterly opposed to the rules and regulations that the government had imposed on Christians in China. Wu also obtained copies of Wang's magazine, *Spiritual Food*. This appointment as Director of the Health Workers Association came to an end in 1953 when Wu was transferred to the Changsha Second Hospital, and then two months later to the Provincial Hospital, also in Changsha.

On January 9, 1956 things took an unexpected and distressing turn. Wu was arrested and put in prison under suspicion of being an anti-revolutionary. This gentle and sensitive man became frightened as guards put handcuffs on his wrists. The shock of this made him visibly shake. Then he experienced a sense of complete peace and well-being. God was going to protect him.

He shared a small cell with a university student who had been given a life sentence for political activities against the government. This fellow prisoner was fluent in Russian, and so Wu decided to make use of his time of confinement by learning this language. He had no Bible or hymn book, and so as he sat in the bare cell he recalled verses and passages with which he was familiar, and sang to himself hymns which he could remember. He wrote them down on paper, and soon had a good repertoire for his private devotions. One day he saw an issue of *Tian Feng*, the magazine of the China Christian Council. There were some hymns in it and some passages of Scripture. He added these to his small collection. He especially loved to sing:

> *Living for Jesus a life that is new,*
> *Striving to please Him in all that I do,*
> *Yielding allegiance, glad-hearted and free,*
> *This is the pathway of blessing for me.*

And he found strength in reciting to himself the words of Jesus:

Blessed *are* they who are persecuted for righteousness' sake: for theirs is the kingdom of heaven (Matthew 5:10, KJV).

His daily routine soon took on a pattern: the early morning was spent in prayer to God, the morning in learning Russian, the afternoon playing chess and poker, and the evening witnessing to his fellow prisoners.

The food in the prison was not good. More precisely, it was quite bad, and it left him with stomach aches. Twice a month his wife brought him food from outside. It was good, nourishing and enjoyable, and this kept him going. But his health begin to deteriorate from the poor quality of the prison food, and one day he hemorrhaged. The warden allowed him to leave prison and go to hospital, from which he later returned to his cell.

In April 1957, after fifteen months of incarceration, Wu was released. He was cleared of the charge that he was an anti-revolutionary, and was classified as an "uncertified person," which meant that he was neither a Communist member nor an anti-revolutionary. Wu emphasizes that he was never beaten or treated roughly while in prison.

Three men who had been imprisoned for their faith and whose friendship Wu had cultivated during this period also gained their liberty. One, after much suffering, had given up his Christian faith. Another, abandoned by his lady friend, committed suicide. A third also rejected his Christian faith. Before this man died, however, he asked his daughter to find Wu and call him to his bedside. There Wu helped him re-commit his life to God. Wu later took the memorial service when this friend died.

In May 1957, just after Wu's release from prison, Mao launched a strong Anti-Rightist campaign aimed at intellectuals who had been critical of the government. Some people were arrested and imprisoned, while others committed suicide. But to his relief Wu realized that following his release and re-instatement he had been given a "clean sheet." Whatever wrongs officialdom had charged him with had been wiped out by his period in prison.

During his imprisonment his wife had been unable to support their three children. The two daughters were sent to live with relatives far from home, while the baby boy, Wu Xingwang, stayed with his mother. Upon Wu's release the two daughters returned home, and it was nice to have the family all together again after two years. Graham Wu worked for one year at the Fourth Hospital of Changsha, which had been recently built. Then he was transferred to a hospital in Zhashe, where a dam was being constructed.

In the rest of China, the Great Leap Forward (1958–1962) had forced millions of town people to work in the countryside growing grain. Mao's grandiose plan had gone horribly wrong, and some 30 million died of malnutrition and famine. But the nature of Wu's specialist work as a doctor had exempted him from joining the trek into the country. For the Wu family this was a period of comfortable living conditions and good food. In his spare time Dr. Wu enjoyed growing vegetables and raising chickens for the family table.

───

By the time the Cultural Revolution began in 1966, Wu was back working in the Changsha Provincial Hospital. The one problem that had arisen at Zashe was that the spray of the dam had affected his wife's arthritis, and this necessitated returning to the capital.

In July 1966 Mao closed down all schools, and commissioned young students to go as Red Guards into the cities to destroy the "Four Olds"—old ideas, old customs, old culture and old habits. At this time Wu had become very vulnerable to Chairman Mao's ideas. He applauded the sending of people of all classes into the countryside to work with their hands. He was impressed with the films and books put out by the Communist party.

He studied *The Thoughts of Chairman Mao*, and conscientiously carried out some self-criticism, and concluded that he had not been a good citizen. Not having been born of a poor family he had been insensitive to the living conditions of the poor. Chairman Mao's books improved his understanding of others, and taught him to behave more considerately to his patients.

Dr. Wu reached a stage, though, where he was trying to combine his Christian faith with Mao's teachings. A hospital leader had warned him that he would face interrogation and questioning about his religious faith and could lose his job. He came to the conclusion that he would stop sharing his faith with others, and only keep it alive in his heart, and in this way avoid trouble. God would help him to keep that inner flame of faith alive, and if pressed he would admit to being a Christian; if that resulted in losing his employment, then so be it.

Soon after the commencement of the Cultural Revolution, Wu had to face an "Accusation Meeting" before a mass of people. He was asked, "Why do you believe in a Western faith? If you don't give a satisfactory answer we will force you to walk down the high street wearing a dunce cap." His unexpected reply was, "Western faiths are not all bad. What about Marxism?" To this the crowds had nothing to say.

This frenzied revolution also included the torturing, maiming and killing of millions of people. People of all ages were beaten with sticks and called insulting names. In one such tussle, Wu saw his secretary being beaten up in front of many onlookers. He shouted out, "Chairman Mao has said, 'Rather use talk in your struggles than fight with weapons.'" His intervention stopped the beating going on, but it also angered some in the crowd. Some friends warned Wu that he would be set upon and they hid him for three days by which time the excitement had died down.

Among the many activities which went on during this danger-ous period was the searching of the homes of suspected dissidents. The Red Army came to Wu's house searching for evidence of anti-government activities. They carried out two searches. The first time they saw that he only had books, and no jewellery or valuables. But the second time they confiscated all his religious books, including his valued two-volumed biography of Hudson Taylor and his Bible, which they took away to destroy. When the soldiers had gone, Wu found that his wife had hidden away a small copy of the New Testament, and he thanked God that they could still read this. This experience taught him how precious the Bible is, and in 1980, when the situation was more open, he resolved to be "God's postman." He would obtain large quantities of Bibles from a large organization, and post them in ones and twos to places in the countryside, where he knew they were badly needed.

Looking back on this ten-year period of "struggle, criticism and transformation" Wu could say that he had never been imprisoned, beaten or separated from his family. He had been able to remain on the premises of his hospital, though he had been demoted from being the senior doctor. He had been forced to do only manual work. In a strange sort of way he enjoyed washing the floors, dusting, cleaning the toilets and waiting on the personal needs of the patients. These routine tasks involved less responsibility.

On the other hand, though, the Cultural Revolution reduced his commitment to his Christian faith. The pressure was intense and unremitting, year after year; he was beginning to believe in the teachings of Chairman Mao. Although initially he had refused to sing songs to Mao, he now began to sing them as freely as everyone else. For advice he turned to the *The Thoughts of Chairman Mao*. He even joined in the widespread worship of Mao early each morning. He justified it to himself by saying that this was not against his Christian faith. He involved his whole family in this routine. Later he confessed that he had made a serious error of judgment, and should not have gone this far.

But better days came in 1978 with Deng Xiaoping at the helm. He began to lead China by a different route of relaxed social conditions and the adopting of an "Open Door" policy. Gone were the arrests, the acrimony and the rigid policies of the previous quarter of a century. A new era was clearly dawning for China.

Wu was most excited. He had submitted to the many prohibitions of the Mao period. Among the many new freedoms he could enjoy was that of being able to read English publications. This included the reading of medical journals, which among other things described the advances of medical science, of which he had heard nothing. Wu had suffered from a severe stomach problem since as far back as 1948. In one article he read of a new method of treating it. He decided that he would be the first "guinea pig" in China. He translated the article into Chinese and reproduced the diagrams, and asked a well-qualified doctor to perform the operation on him. It took six hours of surgery and was a complete success. He in turn wrote an article about this new treatment in a Chinese medical journal so that others could benefit from it. He thanked the Lord for this new environment of freedom, and resolved to follow him without the reservations he had had in recent years.

Another benefit of the new era was government permission to have public worship in church buildings as they were re-opened after thirty years of commercial use. In 1979 Wu heard the wonderful news that the large Mu En Tang church in Shanghai had just been re-opened for worship. During the week it was still being used as a school, but now on Sundays it could be used for religious purposes. He went to the coast and found his way to the spacious building. It was crowded, and the congregation was worshipping with indescribable joy. Wu is not normally an emotional person, but he found himself crying with happiness as he joined in the singing of hymns and listened to the preaching of the Word.

He went to Shanghai again the following year. His old friend Wang Mingdao had just been released after twenty-five years in prison in northwest China, and now had a flat in the city. The elderly pastor admitted to Wu that during the long years in prison he had had periods of doubt about the faith. This comforted Wu,

Dr. Graham Wu (right) pictured with the author, Dr. Norman Cliff,
in Changsha in 1997

who had made some questionable compromises during those
difficult years. While in Shanghai Wu obtained a complete Bible
again after eighteen years with just a New Testament. This was
another bonus given to him by God.

One by one former churches throughout China were being re-opened, having been repaired and refurbished at government expense. In December 1980 the first church in Changsha was opened in the northern part of the city, a former CIM church. Again Wu attended and played his concertina, joining in the celebrations of joy and relief.

Just at this time Wu's work was changed. He was asked to teach English. With Deng's new "Open Door" policy there was an urgent need for people to be able to read and speak English. He could immediately see the many advantages in this change of work. He would have to brush up his knowledge of the language; he would be able to meet with the doctors and staff in a more relaxed atmosphere than in the past; he would not have the anxiety he had had as a surgeon of making fatal mistakes; he would have more time to serve the Lord, and would learn New Testament Greek to improve his understanding of the New Testament.

From 1982 up to the present Wu has been travelling to north China, where he meets Christians in the "underground churches." He has visited groups of forty or fifty believers, and has been deeply moved by their dedication and fervour. He has preached to these peasant believers and has taught them Christian doctrine, and the people have come to love him for his pastoral visits. Attending these "underground" meetings has not been without risk, for there have been times when police have swooped on the gatherings, and made arrests.

His superior at the Changsha hospital, aware of these illegal activities, warned Wu that he could lose his job as a result, but the lay preacher continues to pursue the ministry to which he believes God has called him.

As Graham Wu gets older and less active he has increased the time spent in prayer and intercession in the early hours of each day. He likes to read the story of the times of prayer which led up to the Welsh Revival in the early twentieth century, and the account of prayer gatherings in Korea in the 1940s which brought thousands into the church. He receives much inspiration from the biographies of John Wesley, George Muller and Hudson Taylor, and applies the lessons of their lives to his work for God in Hunan.

On one of my visits to China I was privileged to stay in the home of Wu Guangya and Zhou Yaozhen for four days, and to take part in an informal gathering in their apartment. If I could sum up the secret of Dr. Wu's life it would be in the words of Tennyson:

More things are wrought by prayer
Than this world dreams of.

7

王德潤
DAVID WANG

(WANG DEYUN) 1893–1983

The pastor who removed a picture of Chairman Mao from the wall of his church during a Communist conference

> Whoever wishes to oppose Communism must be prepared to be mauled and torn to pieces by the people. If you have not yet made up your mind about being mauled and torn to pieces, it would be wise for you not to oppose Communism.
> —*Mao Zedong*

David Wang was brought up in a poor home in Jimo, a village in eastern Shandong. His father, a peasant farmer, died when he was small, leaving his mother to bring him up with limited resources. She obtained a loan to send him to the Presbyterian mission school.

His education only started at fourteen. He walked many miles to school in Yantai. But, in spite of this late start, his quick mind, combined with a spirit of determination, soon brought him to the top of the class. At the age of twenty, he was supporting his mother and himself as a teacher.

In his first year at school David Wang made a profession of faith. This brought no opposition from his mother and relatives for he was in fact a fourth-generation Christian. His great grandfather, Wang Weidian, had come into the Christian faith through the evangelistic itinerations of Dr. Hunter Corbett,[1] an American Presbyterian missionary who, with Yantai as his base, travelled every spring and autumn across eastern Shandong, preaching and distributing tracts, and founding churches from small groups of converts.

It was while teaching that he felt the call of God to be a preacher. He went to the recently formed and prestigious Shandong Christian University in Jinan, financed and run by American Presbyterian and British Baptist missionary societies. By arrangement with the principal he spread the four years of theological study over six years so that he could do work on the campus to earn money for his fees and support his widowed mother. He then did a further year of study at Yanjing University in Beijing.

He was now thirty-three years of age, and he took three important steps. First, he married Tong Sumei, a gentle and attractive young lady who lived in the neighbouring village of Zhou Ga Zhuang and had had her education in Penglai. Sumei came from a staunchly Christian home. Her father spent most of his life as a missionary in Manchuria, where thousands of Shandong peasants had migrated after suffering from famine and drought in their home province.

Secondly, Wang was ordained into the Presbyterian ministry and, lastly, he commenced the major work of his life as pastor of a new church in Qingdao, a busy industrial city on the Shandong coast. It was the year 1926 and this new charge was just the challenge that the newly ordained pastor needed. There was no church building and for the first two years he conducted services in a theatre.

The church elders purchased a large piece of ground high up on a hill and on a main road. In slow stages, as the funds became available, building proceeded, with the pastor coming almost daily to watch over every detail. Then the day came when an attractive and utilitarian building was complete. In the basement

---

[1] See also the influence of Dr. Corbett on Fan Peiji in chapter 4.

was the "manse," on the ground floor rooms for Sunday School and nursery classes, and on the first floor the auditorium which could seat 500 people. To Pastor Wang this building was the house of God, the place where God wanted him to preach the words of life to hungry men and women. He resolved to preach faithfully from its pulpit. He was to serve here for a quarter of a century.

By 1937, eleven years after he arrived in Qingdao, there were four children in the family. Michael (Wang Mingli) was born in 1928, Martin (Wang Minglu) in 1934, Mary (Wang Mingyi) in 1935 and Ruby (Wang Mingfan) in 1937. As their father was a pastor as well as a trustee of the mission school, the children were fortunate to have a free education.

On the whole it was a difficult and unsettled time politically. Warlords across north China were competing for spheres of influence. The peasantry, the bulk of Shandong's population, were being exploited by landlords, and little was done to improve their lot by Chiang Kaishek's government. But the governor of Shandong, Han Fuqu, brought a measure of stability and peace to the province in the early 1930s. The annual report of the American Presbyterian mission for 1931 spoke of it as "the happiest year from the standpoint of the political situation which the mission has enjoyed for many years."

But the situation took a dramatic turn for the worse in 1937, when the Japanese commenced a full-scale war in China. Japanese naval units landed in Qingdao on January 10, 1938. The presence of hundreds of Japanese soldiers in the port was resented by the populace, who were aware of the cruelties which these soldiers had practised in Manchuria. Pastor Wang showed no personal hostility to the new arrivals, and taught love and forgiveness in his sermons to his congregation.

A large group of Japanese pastors came to Shandong in the employ of the Japanese Army. They functioned primarily as agents of their country with instructions to put pressure on the churches to form a union, and also to influence the Christians to support their programme of a "New Order in East Asia." Pastor Wang watched the situation in Qingdao carefully as these pastors infiltrated local churches and mission schools, disseminating their propaganda. One student complained that in his school class a Japanese pastor spoke of the Godhead as consisting of four persons—Father, Son, Holy Spirit and the Emperor of Japan.

Wang was a man of goodwill to all and welcomed every contact with Japanese people. His home was frequently visited by a Japanese pastor who was not part of the political programme already described. He was the pastor of a small congregation of Japanese civilians. Pastor Wang was pleased when a Japanese Christian lady doctor and her husband began attending his services. Their love and concern was genuine, for when they learned that the preacher was suffering from malaria they brought to Wang's home some much-needed drugs, as well as some rice at this time of acute shortages. The Wang family were touched by these gestures of kindness and friendship by individual Japanese, but they were nevertheless relieved when at the end of 1945, when the war was over, Japanese troops and civilians were shipped back to Japan.

The end of the eight-year long war, with all its suffering and destruction, brought optimism and hope to Pastor Wang and his church elders. They anticipated that food supplies would improve, that business in the city would stabilize and above all that the churches would be free once again to witness and evangelize. But the bitter fighting between the Kuomintang and Communist forces, which had taken place during the Japanese War, intensified. Believing that the Communists could not do worse than the KMT, the people began to look forward to a change in government.

On June 2, 1949 Qingdao fell into the hands of Communist forces. The stages by which the new government would in the coming years treat the Christian churches was later described in a Lutheran report from this area. First, they gave the assurance that the work of the churches would not be hampered. Then followed the withdrawal of many liberties and the beginning of regimentation. Finally, there was practically no liberty at all.

This is what happened in Qingdao. Pastor Wang was determined to support all that was good in the new programme of improved health and education, but he resolved never to compromise his Christian convictions. He knew that the new authorities would try to woo him, and then use him for their own purposes. There were slogans all over the city lauding the new rulers. On the other hand, people passing through the city told disturbing stories of persecution and suffering under the new regime in other parts of north China. The large congregation began to slowly dwindle. The faith of a few worshippers was insufficiently deep to face the unknown dangers of the future and they stopped church attendance altogether. Others went to small "underground" meetings, while others started having family services in secret.

Pastor Wang had had the habit for some years of publishing a church calendar for the forthcoming year, each issue of which had a special theme. Convinced that suffering and trials lay ahead, he chose the theme for 1951 as "Facing the Cross." This choice proved to be prophetic.

In early December 1950, a year and a half after the Liberation of Qingdao, officials came to Wang's house at the church. They wanted the use of the church building for a conference a few days before Christmas. The pastor made two conditions for the use of the church: no political portraits or flags on the premises and no smoking. While the festivities of Christmas were being celebrated with carol singing, parties and talks on the Saviour's birth, Pastor Wang kept asking himself whether or not he had done the right thing in agreeing to the use of the church. Of course, if he had refused, the authorities would have used the property in any case. The elders agreed with the conditions that he had made. He could only hope and pray that everything would proceed without incident.

But word reached the pastor on the afternoon of the conference that the promised conditions had been flagrantly broken. At the front of the church was a portrait of Chairman Mao with flags on either side of it. Also many in the audience were smoking. Pastor Wang summoned his family into his study and asked them to concentrate in prayer for him. With shaky steps he walked to the door of the church on the first floor of the building. He went up the aisle of the crowded church, removed the portrait of Mao as well as the flags, and walked out.

That incident was to be the turning point in the life of Wang Deyun and that of his family. From that day each member was a marked person in the eyes of the authorities, classified as anti-revolutionaries, enemies, people who could not be trusted. The strongest opposition was focused on the pastor. The local news-papers attacked the Presbyterian minister as being of capitalist and anti-government convictions. At their various schools and colleges the children heard speeches in which their father was harangued anonymously.

One further development forced the pastor to take serious stock of his position. A fellow pastor warned him that on January 6, 1951 there was to be an "Accusation Meeting" against him in a large park, at which local pastors would be called upon to accuse him of ten charges listed by the authorities. However much they loved him they would have to give carefully prepared speeches that would be satisfactory to the organizers. If they refused their lives and those of their families would be in danger.

After private discussion with Michael, his eldest child, Wang decided that, in order to save his fellow pastors from undue pressure he would have to disappear from the city. On the night of January 2 when his family was sleeping the pastor left the city and travelled south. As Mary, his daughter, later recalled, "We

Pastor David Wang pictured in 1951 with his wife Tong Sumei (left), his sister, and his children. From left: Ruby, Martin, Michael, Mary.

went to bed and he was there. We got up the next morning and he was missing." When Mrs. Wang was asked by officials of her husband's whereabouts she said in all honesty that she did not know—likewise with the children at college and school.

Soon afterwards Michael was given a tip-off by a university friend that, in view of his father's absence, he would have to stand trial on the due date. Furthermore, this friend himself had been instructed to be his accuser. They mutually agreed that Michael should also leave the city and go into hiding. This would save both of them having to take part in this potentially dangerous situation.

The following day Michael rode to university as usual, attended his normal lectures and at 4 p.m. rode to the railway station. There he met a fellow Christian student, with whom he exchanged his bicycle for the purchasing of a ticket to Shanghai and some food. While on the train he wondered how he would find his father who had preceded him to Shanghai.

Upon arrival there he went directly to the offices of the Church of Christ in China. When he got there he entered the office just as the General Secretary and his father were rising from prayer. Pastor Wang was taken aback to see his son. They stayed in the home of a distant relative, and for several days tried to make plans as to what to do next. The pastor finally persuaded Michael that they should return to Qingdao, where his son would hand him over to the authorities.

Just at this time, Pastor Wang's sister, a church worker in Qingdao, had a vivid dream that her brother was in Shanghai in desperate need of funds to go south. She packed all her savings of gold and caught a train to the metropolis. But how was she to find her brother in this vast city? To her surprise she spotted Pastor Wang and Michael standing in a queue to buy tickets to return home to Qingdao.

What this lady said to them settled the question with which they had been grappling for several days. "God has told me in a dream," she said, "to give you these funds to enable you to go south." The two then bought tickets to go to Canton, while the sister returned to Qingdao. The political situation at that time was such that on the journey south the passengers were uncommunicative with each other. No stranger could be trusted. Some were no doubt fleeing from arrest by the authorities, while others might be informers listening for vital information to report.

Father and son arrived at Canton, planning to proceed to Hong Kong. They found a Christian church, also affiliated to the Church of Christ in China. The pastor was abrupt with them and was afraid to be involved in their situation. This attitude he slightly modified when Pastor Wang pointed to a picture on his wall in which the two of them were standing, one in front of the other, at a church conference in Suzhou. The local pastor agreed that they could sleep in the church that night, provided that they moved on the next day.

God's messengers seemed to be meeting them at each juncture. As they were settling down for the night in the cold building, a visitor joined them and listened to their story, and promised to help them get to Hong Kong. It was just the time of year when students in Canton could travel home for the Chinese New Year celebrations. Students in the Christian Union at the local university, knowing Michael's name and the story of his experience at the Qingdao University, readily agreed to escort them as they went home for the New Year's Christian conference.

During the four-hour train journey father and son hurriedly learned some basic Cantonese, the only test at that time for entry into Hong Kong. But at the border Pastor Wang's mind went blank, and he could not say a word of the dialect. He was refused entry, and so he returned to Shenzhen with Michael and a pastor's son who knew the area well. In a farmhouse the two changed into peasant clothing, and some experienced guides took them in the dark to Shenzhen where they were carried across a narrow river, assisted up a steep and high hill, through a gap in the fencing across the border.

The two men arrived in the British colony on January 26, 1951 with few contacts and ignorant of their directions in the Hong Kong streets, but one opening after another came to them. Michael found some casual employment, and the pastor found rewarding work under the Christian and Missionary Alliance among the thousands of refugees who had fled from the mainland, of which he himself was one!

The pastor asked himself if he had done God's will in making this sudden break from his fruitful ministry in Qingdao. Those whom he had left behind in China would be the victims of the harsh regime, constantly being interrogated as to his whereabouts. In a circuitous way a letter from Michael reached the family in Qingdao, indicating that they were both safe and out of the country.

And what of the family left behind? One by one they were able to reach Hong Kong safely over a period of the following six years. In 1953 eighteen-year-old Mary became a medical student at the large First Medical College of Shanghai, set in beautiful surroundings. She studied hard and maintained the faith, though under constant pressure to deny her Christian beliefs. During the week she met for prayer early each morning on the roof of a pharmacy with a group of courageous fellow students. On Sundays she drew inspiration from Watchman Nee's preaching at the Little Flock Assembly in Nanyang Road. Under her pillow she had a translation of Roy Hession's *The Calvary Road,* which she found particularly relevant to her current situation.

Soon after Mary's arrival in Shanghai she followed up a contact of her brother Michael's and met a widow at the Little Flock church, who kindly offered to board her mother and sister Ruby in her home. The following year, in 1954, Mrs. Wang suffered from increasingly poor health. After many failed attempts Mary eventually obtained an exit visa for her mother to leave the country. She was able to join her husband, Pastor Wang, after three and a half years of separation. Ruby could only go as far as Canton, and studied in a boarding school there. Two years later, in 1957, she was allowed to leave for Hong Kong. Michael met her and took her to the British colony. Now four members of the family were together in Hong Kong.

We return to the story of Mary. During a summer vacation a female medical student in her class was paired off with her 24 hours a day to exert pressure on her to give up her Christian faith. But, she firmly maintained her loyalty to Christ. Mary recalls, "She believed that Communism would conquer the world in her lifetime, and this belief was her whole motivation." But the harsh environment of propaganda and slogans, of thought reform and periods of self-criticism began to wear Mary down. Imagine the anxiety her family in Hong Kong had when receiving a letter from her in March 1956, which said:

I have started to distinguish between what is the real faith in Christ, and what are the teachings which are harmful to China...I must not allow anyone to be under the protection of the Christian faith who makes serious criticisms of the new system.

A year later Mary was given a visa to visit her family. But all the way from Shanghai to Hong Kong she was accompanied by a male medical student, obviously selected by the authorities to keep a close watch on her. When Michael met them at Hong Kong it proved difficult to shake off this student who was determined to ascertain her address in the colony and keep a watch on her activities.

Mary firmly intended this visit to be temporary, as she was keen to complete her medical studies and become a doctor. Her parents pressed her to stay and she resisted. But finally through a vivid dream she felt that God was telling her to remain. Pastor and Mrs. Wang, Michael, Mary and Ruby were now finally together in Hong Kong.

And what of Martin, the only one still in China? He studied at a college in Qingdao and joined its strong and active Christian Union. The atmosphere on campus was such that they met on a hillside for prayer every morning at 5:30 a.m. Nearly a hundred attended, and in the dark they had intensive Bible study and times of prayer, asking God for courage to keep faith with him. In 1954 the police swooped down on this group and the leaders were arrested, never to return. Martin later learned that they had been placed in one of the dreaded reform-through-labour camps (*lao gai*).

When Martin graduated as an architect he was sent to work on a building project in northern Manchuria, building three large factories. There he worked from 1954 to 1958, and during this time he was able to send money to his family in Qingdao and Shanghai. At that time the workers in China worked seven days a week with no day of rest. Martin kept his faith alive by secretly reading his pocket New Testament during his daily midday break. When he heard by letter that his mother had had a stroke he obtained an exit visa to visit her. His work unit (*dan wei*) record had no mention of his family's activities nor of his own at college, so, with no blots on his record, he got the visa without delay. He decided to stay in Hong Kong. The family was now complete, united in their desire to continue serving the Lord.

Pastor Wang worked for the Christian and Missionary Alliance in Hong Kong from 1951 to 1968, when with his wife he joined Martin and Mary in London. They were then invited to serve a Chinese congregation in Paris for a year before retiring. He died in London in 1983. Mrs. Wang had died nine years earlier. Michael worked as a lift engineer and emigrated in 1974 to Australia, where he started a Chinese church. After four years in Hong Kong, Mary went to London where for a third of a century she has been doing a fruitful work under the Chinese Overseas Christian Mission (COCM) among many of her fellow country-men in Britain and Europe. This has grown into a large work with an ambitious programme of evangelism and church planting.

Martin worked as a civil engineer in Hong Kong, and came to Britain in 1965, where he initially worked as an architect and then went into business on his own. He retired in 1985. For over thirty years he has helped in the COCM work in London, and assisted many worthy Christian organizations. Martin has given financial support to the training of seminary students in his native Shandong. Ruby, after working as a teacher in Hong Kong, went to Britain in 1979, where she has also joined the COCM, and where she is manager of its book room.

As a family they have been through many trials and tribula-tions, but all have given their skills and time to the building up of the kingdom of God among their own people. As a family they could testify to the truth of Paul's declaration:

> I have become absolutely convinced that neither Death nor Life, neither messenger of heaven nor monarch of earth,

neither what happens today nor what may happen tomor-
row, neither a power from on high nor a power from below,
nor anything else in God's whole world has any power to
separate us from the love of God in Jesus Christ our Lord!
(Romans 8:38–39, J.B. PHILLIPS)

8

王鎮
WANG ZHEN

1910–1983

The man who solemnly kept his promise to God

> Has the Lord Almighty been defeated? Are the labours of thousands of missionaries in vain? And what about the prayers of the saints? Ever since the takeover of China God's children have prayed for the day when the Lord would deliver His own on the mainland. Were they all beating the air? No! Absolutely not!
> —Silas Hong in *The Dragon Net*

At the age of seventeen, young Wang Zhen became a member of the Communist Youth League. In schools, offices and workshops lectures and discussions were being held on the virtues of Marxism. On the streets of his native town in Zhangjiakou in northern Hebei placards poked fun at the declining power of Chiang Kaishek.

Better living conditions, assistance to the farmers, education for all—it made sense. To belong to this new fast-growing movement brought with it excitement, action and also turmoil. The young man joined in all the activities with gusto.

But in the following two years the Kuomintang (the Chinese Nationalist Party) liquidated hundreds of Communist Party members. Others were held in prison, where two thirds of them recanted. Wang Zhen now knew that his life was in danger and so he decided to disappear until the crisis was over. In fact, to ensure his survival in future years, he severed all links with the Party.

The year 1930, when he turned twenty, was a critical period for him. He developed some distressing physical symptoms, and it looked as though he might die. He had an infection in one foot that spread to his leg. It became dangerously swollen and the illness left him thin and weak. He had difficulty doing his daily manual work. It was in the days before antibiotics and so it was almost impossible to find the right treatment. One day a German doctor examined him, and explained that in order to survive he would have to have the leg amputated. This came as a shock to both Wang and his parents.

When the doctor gave Wang Zhen's mother a form to sign agreeing to the operation, she refused to comply. She said that she would rather trust God to bring healing. Wang agreed with his mother, though he did not profess faith in God. In his state of discomfort from his swollen leg he made a promise to God that if his leg was cured he would serve him all his life. This is a vow so often made in life's crises, but so easily forgotten when all is well again.

One day soon afterwards, the young man felt new power pulsating through his body. His infection went and his health began to steadily improve. He became a Christian and remembered the promise he had made to God. His life now had a new purpose—to work and live for God. In his bedroom he hung up on the wall a painting of Christ on the cross. On either side of the picture were the words of John 3:16, and this became his message as he began to preach in his own simple way in and around Zhangjiakou in Hebei.

In 1931 a Pentecostal missionary, Mr. H.E. Hansen, arrived in the town from Stockholm, Sweden. He heard the young man's story and immediately took a keen interest in him. Later he suggested that Wang equip himself for the ministry, and go to the North China Theological Seminary in Beijing. Wang benefited greatly from the lectures he attended, and threw himself into preparing himself to be a preacher of the gospel. It was while he was studying here that the Bethel Worldwide Evangelistic Band had special meetings in the capital. The principal speaker was John Sung (Song Shangjie), and Wang was captivated by his powerful preaching. Here was a Chinese addressing Chinese, and the response to his preaching was greater than he had previously witnessed.

These meetings had a twofold effect on Wang Zhen. First, and most important of all, he received new spiritual life and power in himself. Song's sermons brought content to the faith that he had embraced at his conversion. Secondly, to see hundreds of men and women making professions of faith excited the young Bible student, and gave him a vision of what could be done if a preacher spoke in the power of the Holy Spirit. He resolved to preach and teach in this way in his future ministry.

Upon his graduation in 1934, Wang returned to his native Zhangjiakou to preach to his own people. A year later he was asked to become vice-principal of the Truth Bible Institute of the Assemblies of God in Zhu Shi Avenue, Beijing. His main subject was the Pauline Epistles. This important work of training others for Christian service lasted four happy years. He then became the editor of the Assemblies of God magazine, *Faith and Victory*. Meanwhile he was preaching in and around Beijing. This developed into an itinerant ministry in many provinces, going as far south as Zhejiang and Fujian, and as far north as Mongolia.

By now Wang Zhen had a family of seven children. His wife Liu Muzhen was always glad when he returned home to do his work of preparing sermons and material for *Faith and Victory*. His study consisted of a bed, cupboard, table and a pile of theological books. On the wall was his much-loved picture of Christ on the cross. As he sat there preparing articles and sermons, and answering correspondence his children would gather around him and ask him all kinds of questions. He enjoyed telling them Bible stories and giving them instruction in the faith. His daughter

Wang Aiyi recalled to me:

> He told us to live honest and pure lives, and to remember to
> thank God for all his blessings. One of his favourite verses
> was "Faith without works is dead" (James 2:26). By this he
> meant that we must show what we believe by the way we
> live. He also liked to quote Ephesians 4:1: "Walk worthy of
> your calling."

She also remarked:

> I always liked to hear him preach. He did it systematically
> and expressed profound truths in simple words. Everyone
> could understand him. His illustrations and stories made his
> messages all the clearer.

The bombing of Pearl Harbor by Japan in December 1941 and
the consequent declaration of war on Japan by America and
Britain brought drastic changes to Christian work in China, as
we have seen. Some missionaries left their stations immediately
to return to their home countries, while others were later
interned in Japanese civilian camps.

An American missionary called Mary Stephany had been running
an orphanage of fifty children in Dachang in northeast Shanxi, as
well as a small home for elderly widows. In this work she was
assisted by two other colleagues, Henrietta Tieleman and Alice
Stewart. Many were the moving stories which Mary Stephany
could tell of finding babies (mostly girls) in such places as garbage
bins and in the long grass, barely alive and crying pitifully. With no
knowledge of who their parents were she would take them into the
loving care of her orphanage.

One day soon after the declaration of war by the United States,
a Japanese officer gave Mary Stephany and her colleagues notice

that they must prepare immediately to leave for an internment camp in Shandong. Just at that time Pastor Wang Zhen had been preaching in Dachang. The lady missionary saw this as God's provision, and pleaded with the pastor to take over the running of the orphanage after the missionaries left. This came as a surprise to the young man. He had had no experience of this kind of work, and he knew that with the escalating war there would be all kinds of problems. He took several days to make his decision. Guidance came through Wang reminding himself that God is the God of widows and orphans, and that in taking over this work he would be serving such a God.

On June 7, 1942 two Japanese officers escorted the lady missionaries out of the mission compound. Wang Zhen was now in charge. He was thirty-two years of age, and would be responsible for the protection and support of some seventy people of all ages, as well as his own large family.

The first problem that he faced was the discontinuance of funds from the USA, the source of financial support for the previous twenty years. When he had settled into the new work he asked God how he could lead this work with no more foreign funds coming in. While he was praying two ideas came to him, which he believed were from God.

First, he would arrange for the older children to be taught knitting and embroidery, and the completed items could be sold to support the work. Second, he would travel around the provinces in north China, and ask Christians to make donations to the work, and whatever he also received for preaching would go into the funds. These ideas were successful and the charitable work done in Christ's name was maintained in this way.

Once, in between Wang's journeys to preach and solicit donations, he saw a Japanese soldier at the front door. There was a menacing look on his face and the pastor sensed danger. When he opened the door the soldier shouted at him in Japanese and stabbed him, pushing past him into the orphanage, where he grabbed some food from the home's limited supplies and departed. Fortunately the wound was not deep and Wang recovered, and was able to continue his work. There were also times when local gangs tried to plunder the orphanage, as food in the village was in critically short supply, and Wang Zhen had to plead with them not to steal from his limited resources. In spite of dangerous incidents such as these, Wang Zhen was able to maintain the work with which the American missionary had entrusted him throughout the protracted war.

The superintendency of the Dachang Orphanage revealed Wang's many talents. He was the odd-jobs man, repairing the property whenever it was needed. He was the home's tailor, making clothes both for his own family and his extended family. Above all, he was a loving father to these children, who had been rejected and thrown out by their parents in babyhood, and had known little love. He would spend time with the orphans individually, holding them tenderly on his knee. He knew the personal background of each one of them. There was the little baby girl whom his daughter Aiyi had found on the steps of the local temple, with a card pinned to her clothes asking for help. Aiyi gladly brought her to the home in the mission compound. There was the baby boy found inside a box in a field. Passersby heard his pathetic cry and brought him to the home.

The children liked to express their love for their pastor by singing a song of gratitude:

> *You nourished our lives which had been rejected.*
> *This is indeed a blessing from God.*
> *This is the work God called you to do.*
> *Listen! Can you hear a baby cry?*
> *As you see us in the classroom*
> *Can you see the love of God in us?*
> *We in turn wish to be channels of blessing to others.*

Pastor Wang Zhen took over the superintendency of the Dachang Orphanage after the American missionaries running it were removed by Japanese officers in 1942. Wang was later to spend twenty-five years in a reform-through-labour camp at Hadan in Hebei.

Pastor Wang was careful to stress that it was God's love in his heart that had done this work, not his own.

In 1948, three years after the Japanese War was over, Wang Zhen moved his orphans to Beijing. The numbers were now down, for some who were now past childhood stayed in the Dachang Christian community. Those who went with Wang were no longer small children. They had become part of his family and when the group arrived in the capital he resolved to get each young person the best possible education. Through gifts received from local Christians he was able to send them to the best schools in Beijing, though he still had to make personal contributions himself. He liked to sing a hymn based on our Lord's words in Matthew 6:25–30:

> *Birds in the sky, flowers on the ground.*
> *Who cares for them?*
> *Then will he not care about my needs?*
> *My soul looks up to the Lord, who has*
> *   shown infinite love to me.*
> *He died for me, He forgave my sins.*
> *My life rests on the Lord's care and guidance,*
> *So I need not worry.*

The early years after Liberation in 1949 were difficult ones for church leaders. They knew that the rank and file of church members looked to them for guidance. The preachers had always taught them in their sermons that they must obey Christ before all other human allegiances, including the government if it conflicted with our Lord's teaching. Christians must be ready to take up the cross and follow Christ regardless of the consequences, they had asserted.

It had all sounded so straightforward, so black and white. But no one could have anticipated what form the new situation under

Chairman Mao would take or how close to home the demands now being promulgated by the new rulers would come. When they were advancing towards the capital Communist soldiers had been friendly, efficient and even concerned about the welfare of the ordinary peasants, the people who had felt so neglected by the Kuomintang government.

But word soon got around the small communities of Christians in north China that a dozen of the most respected leaders had met at the Tabernacle of Wang Mingdao in Shijia Hutong, Beijing. They had met to discuss how to respond to the pressure put on them to join and support the newly formed Three Self Patriotic Movement. They had come to a unanimous conclusion. To join the TSPM at that time would be to compromise. How could the church be subject to an atheistic government? Christianity is essentially a spiritual movement, and the TSPM was a political organization with which they could not co-operate in any way.

So compliant had some churches in Beijing become under the new regime that in their services they were singing the popular song to Mao Zedong:

> *From the red East rises the sun,*
> *In China appears Mao Zedong.*
> *He works for the people's welfare,*
> *He is the people's great saviour.*
>
> *The Communist party is like the sun,*
> *Wherever it shines there is light.*
> *Wherever the Communist party goes*
> *There the people are liberated.*

By contrast, at Wang Mingdao's Tabernacle, a thousand voices were singing lustily:

> *How sweet the name of Jesus sounds*
> *In a believer's ear.*
> *It soothes his sorrows, heals his wounds*
> *And drives away his fear.*

This large austere-looking building had become a rallying point for all who had misgivings about the new regime.

Pastor Wang Zhen was a personal friend of Wang Mingdao, and a staunch supporter of this movement of non-conformity and non-co-operation. He was not one who could keep his deeply held convictions to himself, and he sometimes voiced his opinions rather strongly. It was not long before his blunt words reached the ears of the authorities. For some months Wang Zhen had realized that his outspokenness would end up with his going to jail. It was only a question of when. So he had developed the habit of always having a toothbrush in his pocket in readiness of being arrested at any time.

In 1955, most of the small group who had met privately at the Tabernacle were arrested. As feared, Wang Zhen's turn came. Initially he was put in a prison north of Beijing, where he passed the long hours of each day making baskets. Then he was sent to do hard labour in a reform-through-labour prison at Handan in Hebei.

The work in the fields was heavy, and the hours worked were long. The positive side of it was that he now had time while doing his routine work to pray, to meditate and to take stock of his life. Pastor Wang had a gift for expressing himself in poetry. So he used the tiniest piece of paper on which to write some verse. He wrote in a code that he had formulated so that the authorities would not know what he had written. He folded the small piece of paper into minute squares and hid it in his socks. He wanted to show these verses one day to his family, and did not want his guards to understand them.

Wang Zhen worked month after month, year after year, under the blazing sun and with blistered hands. He looked back at his past life as he laboured in the fields. He had called on God to heal him when his leg was septic and his prayer had been answered. He had looked after the orphans and widows after his missionary friends had left for America, and God had supplied their needs. He had preached in many provinces of his motherland, and God had used his humble efforts to present the gospel. He reflected that the God who had helped him in all these varied circumstances would surely help him through these days of hard labour.

Wang was now getting older—he was fast approaching the age of seventy. After the many years of living and working in a *lao gai* his health was beginning to deteriorate. He had diabetes and sometimes fainted while working. His leg was swollen once again and it became difficult to walk. In 1979, aged sixty-nine, Wang was taken to a hospital in Beijing. He was kept under constant surveillance.

While he was lying in the hospital, a message reached him. Could he help with preaching in a registered church where the pastors were short-staffed? His immediate reaction was negative. He had spent twenty-four years in prison suffering for his convictions about not joining the official church. How could he now go back on all that?

But events took an unexpected turn and perhaps God was in it. An old woman, who had known him well in earlier years, came to see him and said, "I have been praying all these years for your release so that you can serve the churches. Now that you have had this invitation you just cannot turn it down." Then his children, now grown up, came to see him. He was almost a stranger to them, but they were overjoyed to visit him after all the years of separation. They pleaded with their father saying, "If God has called you to preach, how can you turn this opportunity down? At least we will be able to see you again."

These two incidents touched the seventy-year-old preacher deeply, and made him realize that God was guiding him to do the unexpected. In 1980 he came out of the hospital and jail, and joined the pastoral team at the Gangwashi Church in west Beijing. He now preached with fervour and with a purpose, to give the few remaining years of his life to God's service. The verse in the Bible that came to him was, "...unless a kernel of wheat falls to the ground and dies, it remains only a single seed. But if it dies, it produces many seeds" (John 12:24, NIV).

Wang was determined in the time left to him to produce seeds that would bear fruit. He also thought of the words of Paul in the last letter he wrote, "Preach the Word; be prepared in season and out of season" (2 Timothy 4:2a, NIV).

The elderly man began to preach to passersby in Rice Market Avenue. He found that the people were hungry for the Word of God. They would stop and listen and a crowd would gather. The traffic could not move. The response of the authorities was gentler than Wang expected. The harsh day of arrests seemed to have gone. They referred the preacher to the large Chong Wen Men Church at the centre of the city, and within those four walls he was free to teach and preach. He was now preaching at two of Beijing's large churches.

Had he gone back on the resolution made many years earlier, namely that under no circumstances would he ever work with the TSPM? In fact he had, but so much had changed since those early years of the "Accusation Meetings" and harsh regulations about worship. He felt that both he had changed and the movement had changed with the passing of the years. The once tense relationship between the churches and the government-controlled Religious Affairs Bureau had stabilized. No longer were songs compliantly sung in church services to Chairman Mao, who had by now died and been succeeded by Deng Xiaoping, who was leading a much more flexible regime. The church had learned to live under a Marxist government. Wang now felt free to preach in official churches, provided he could do so without interference.

For some three years Wang had the satisfaction of preaching the gospel once again as he had done in the days of his youth in other parts of north China. But the hardships in the *lao gai* were catching up with him. He was suffering from heart trouble and diabetes, and there were times when he could do nothing more than lie in bed reading his favourite book in the Bible—the Epistle to the Romans.

Looking back on his life with its varied experiences he could heartily affirm Paul's doxology in Romans:

> Oh, the depth of the riches of the wisdom and the
>   knowledge of God!
> How unsearchable his judgments,
> and his paths beyond tracing out!
> "Who has known the mind of the Lord?
> Or who has been his counselor?"
> "Who has ever given to God, that God should repay him?"
> For from him and through him and to him are all things.
> To him be the glory forever! Amen.
> (Romans 11:33–36, NIV)

After many months of illness and weakness, Wang Zhen went to his eternal reward on November 12, 1983.

9

A NEW LONG MARCH

Looking to the future

> *We may not count her armies, we may not see her King;*
> *Her fortress is a faithful heart, her pride is suffering.*
> *And soul by soul, and silently, her shining bounds*
>   *increase;*
> *Her ways are ways of gentleness and all her paths*
>   *are peace.*
> —Cecil Spring-Rice

In the late 1970s, as part of his "Open Door Policy," Deng Xiaoping announced that he would lead the Chinese nation on a "New Long March" towards the twenty-first century. He was referring to the Four Modernizations of his programme to update agriculture, industry, science and technology, and defence. At the time the *Peking People's Daily* took up his programme with enthusiasm and stated:

> The Chinese people's march towards the great goal of the Four Modernizations echoes from the foothills of the Yenshan mountains, to the shores of the Yellow Sea, to all corners of the world, and has aroused worldwide attention. We are setting

out to conquer on our New Long March the mountains, seas, plains, oil fields and mines of our motherland.

The Chinese church is also involved in a New Long March. The heroes of the faith described in this book, and countless others like them who have also kept the faith will soon have all passed on. A new generation of Christian soldiers is assuming the leadership and marching into the future. In my visits I have met some of them and caught something of their fervour and vision.

They will not have to face another Cultural Revolution under which their predecessors had to suffer, but there is no way of knowing what ups and downs lie ahead as they march forward together into the new century. Only God knows that.

As the title of this book suggests, *fierce may be the conflict* in the coming years. Frances Ridley Havergal says:

> *Fierce may be the conflict,*
> *Strong may be the foe,*
> *But the King's own army*
> *None can overthrow.*

It is also true that Christ's army of soldiers will not be able to march "from the foothills of the Yenshan mountains to the shores of the Yellow Sea." The laws of the land preclude them from marching geographically across China, but march they will. I was told some time ago that 30,000 Chinese become Christians every day. Perhaps the figure is higher now. That may seem a drop in the bucket in view of China's population of 1.26 billion people. But if we consider the fact that on January 1, 1800 there was not a single Christian in China and that today there are some 50 million Christians there, that has taken some marching!

As Cecil Spring-Rice says, "soul by soul." Does not that describe the steady growth of God's church in China?

The New Long March of the church began in the dark days of

the Cultural Revolution of 1966 to 1976. We in the West thought it was the beginning of the end. A secular writer said in 1958 when the Denunciation Meetings were in progress and the Cultural Revolution had not even begun, "Whether the Christianity nurtured by 120 years of missionary effort in China will survive this hostile environment remains to be seen."

A former missionary to China wrote in 1974, when the proletarian Cultural Revolution had been proceeding for eight years:

> Although it is obvious that Christianity has not yet died out, and indeed is far from moribund, at present there are no grounds for certainty that the historical fruits of past missionary work will not ultimately largely or completely disappear. To think otherwise is to ignore the lessons of the past.

But, unknownst to us at the time, Christians were meeting in thousands of home meetings. They were being joined by many Chinese who had become disillusioned with Maoism. When the Cultural Revolution petered out in 1976, the exciting news reached us in the West that the church in China could now be numbered in millions. The New Long March had begun.

Churches which had been used by the government as offices, factories and warehouses, were renovated and handed back to the Christian communities. To the surprise of the authorities they have been filled every Sunday by thousands of worshippers since their re-opening.

When Paul was in prison and writing his Epistle to the church at Philippi, he wanted to show the Christians that even this confinement which hindered him from preaching and spreading the gospel was part of God's plan. He said, "I would ye should understand, brethren, that the things *which happened* unto me have fallen out rather unto the furtherance of the gospel" (Philippians 1:12, KJV).

Had there been no Cultural Revolution, even with all the

suffering which Christians underwent during it, there would not have been the conversions and growth of the Christian movement in China.

As J.R. Lowell says:

> *Truth for ever on the scaffold,*
> *Wrong for ever on the throne.*
> *Yet that scaffold sways the future,*
> *And, behind the dim unknown*
> *Standeth God within the shadow,*
> *Keeping watch above His own.*

Appendix i

SMOOTH STONES

A sermon by Pastor Wang Mingdao[1]

> [David] took his staff in his hand, and chose him five smooth stones out of the brook, and put them in a shepherd's bag (1 Samuel 17:40a, KJV).

All readers of the Old Testament are familiar with the story of David and Goliath. Goliath was the champion of the Philistines, and he was feared by the whole army of Israel. Yet David killed him, and so delivered the people of Israel from the Philistines. He did it with one small stone. Strange! Truly strange!

The potential of one small stone was so great that it could achieve deliverance for all the people of Israel. Obviously an important factor in this achievement was the skill of David in slinging stones. But most important of all was the fact that this was a marvellous act of God. For, in effecting this deliverance, God needed only one small stone to kill the champion—the fierce champion from whom everybody fled in fear. Similarly, when God effects deliverance today He can use even the weakest of believers to achieve that which, without Him, would be impossible, even for an army.

---

[1] The preacher who had much influence over Allen Yuan. From *A Stone Made Smooth* [trans. Arthur Reyonolds] (Southampton: Mayflower Christian Books, 1981), 240–245. Used with kind permission of Mayflower Christian Books.

The people around David were under the impression that only the use of the sword, spear and javelin could defeat a powerful enemy. But God made use of what man overlooked—a stone. Nowadays there is a common impression that only people with learning, ability, position and wealth can achieve anything great. But God uses believers who are foolish, weak, poor and lowly to do wonderful things for Him. Paul says, "God hath chosen the foolish things of the world to confound the wise; and God hath chosen the weak things of the world to confound the things which are mighty. And base things of the world, and things which are despised, hath God chosen, *yea*, and things which are not, to bring to nought things that are: that no flesh should glory in his presence" (1 Corinthians 1:27–29, KJV). God could do wonderful things like this in days of old. He can do wonderful things today. He alone is worthy to be praised.

At the same time we are confronted here with a certain factor which we must not lightly dismiss. It is that when God used David to kill Goliath, the stones that David used were not ordinary stones. They were "smooth stones" specially selected from the brook. Now the stones which lay in the brook were far too numerous to be counted. Yet only a few of them were suitable for David's sling.

Before David could go to the field of battle he had to make his way first to the brook, and from the thousands of stones which lay there to select five smooth stones for his sling. He had to aim accurately and to hit the enemy's forehead. The stones had to be smooth. We must remember, however, that the process of making these stones smooth enough for use could not be compressed into a day. On the contrary it would require years and years of preparation.

The stones which we find in brooks or on the seashore were originally thrown out as a result of huge explosions among the rocks. But all these stones at that time had sharp edges and corners. Not one of them was smooth. But as the flowing water swept over them they were constantly colliding with each other, and constantly rubbing each other. In this way the corners were gradually rubbed off. As the process continued for thousands of years the stones in time became perfectly smooth.

Now we often pick up stones like this both from streams and from the seashore. But do we ever stop to think of the long process of friction which has made them smooth? The more these stones were thrown together the more their corners were worn off and the smoother they became. At the same time they became more beautiful and more useful. Since stones are inanimate objects they have no feeling, and naturally we never associate the process of smoothing with pain. But if stones had feeling when they were in collision with each other for such a long time I honestly do not know to what degree their suffering would extend.

The people whom God chooses and uses are in a similar situation. They have been saved, and the sins of the past have been forgiven, but many corners remain in their makeup. There are things like laxity, pride, selfishness, covetousness, envy and hatred. Unless their corners are submitted to a long process of rubbing and buffeting they will not easily be removed.

The question arises, what does God make use of to carry out this process of rubbing? He uses the people around us. That which continually rubs and polishes a stone is not soil, sand, bricks, or pieces of wood; even less is it grass, leaves, cotton wadding or sheep's wool. None of these things is hard like the stone. And none of them will ever rub off the corners. The stones are made smooth because they are constantly rubbed by other stones—vast numbers of them. Only hard things can wear out hard things. When the mountain torrents catch up the small stones and sweep them together they gradually lose their corners.

In the same way, for the corners in our personalities to be rubbed off we need to be thrown together with other people. I buffet you, and you buffet me. By nature we like to live with people who are meek, peaceable, humble, patient, compassionate and benevolent. But God seems to go out of his way, as it were, to put us in the midst of people who are evil, violent, proud, irritable, self-centred and cruel. We murmur against God for not treating us more kindly. We lament that our lot is unpleasant, and we long to get release from our situation.

We fail to perceive that God has purposely placed us in the midst of people like this so that the corners in our personalities, of which he is well aware, may in the course of time be rubbed completely off. Without treatment like this the corners will remain. If you put a small stone with edges and corners into a ball of cotton wadding, even if it remains there for hundreds of years, the corners will not be worn down in the slightest. In the same way, if we live always among virtuous people our corners will remain with us—even perhaps until the Lord returns.

We often wonder why God persists in keeping us in unpleasant surroundings, in making us mix with unattractive people. For instance, a man by nature wishes to take a wife who is virtuous, wise and submissive, yet contrary to his wishes the wife he marries is fierce and excitable. A woman by nature wishes to be married to a man who is gentle and considerate, but contrary to her desire she finds herself married to one who is churlish and rude. An elderly woman looks for a daughter-in-law who is filial and dutiful. But, contrary to her hopes, her son takes a wife who has no respect for her superiors. A young wife hopes to have a kindly mother-in-law, but she finds her husband's mother to be unreasonable and truculent. Masters desire employees who are loyal and obedient, but those they take on prove to be deceitful, cunning and depraved. Employees wish to work for kind and considerate masters, but find that they are cruel and repressive. Landlords fail to find good tenants, and tenants fail to find good landlords. Senior government officials cannot find good subordinates, and subordinate officials look in vain for suitable superiors.

So the general situation is most unsatisfactory. Reality rarely matches the ideal. God appears to be hostile to us, and to be purposely loading us with trouble. But as soon as we understand the significance of the smooth stones our many complaints then vanish. Some of the people in our families are hard to get along with, and some of the people who share our courtyards are hard to live with. But God has expressly placed us among them so that they may help to rub off our edges and corners. In this situation all that we can do is to maintain thankful and obedient hearts, and to endure the inevitable buffeting, so that in the end we become like smooth stones. We shall then be of great potential and usefulness to the Lord.

Even though people might treat us roughly, once we have understood the significance of the stones we shall cease to complain against God. No more shall we choose to get out of our situation or seek to avoid the people who do not appeal to us. We accept God's perfect will, and endure what he sends so that he can make us into smooth stones all the sooner. The pain which prolonged buffeting brings to us may be intense, but the advantages we gain by paying this price are such as can never be bought by silver or gold.

There are so many stones in the brook that you cannot count them. Yet in every ten you cannot find more than one or two that are usable. There was no room in David's pouch for the stones which had not been polished smooth. The process of attrition was essential. In the same way those believers who have not yet experienced trials and afflictions, and who have not yet been disciplined by God, are still not yet ready for his use.

We have seen then that David had to select five smooth stones from the brook before he went out to do battle. The question now before me is whether God, from this great gathering of believers, can choose five who are polished, smooth and prepared, like the five stones of David. What I am even more anxious to know is whether I myself am qualified *to be a "smooth stone" in the hand of God.*

Appendix ii

THE PATH OF PROGRESS
—PRESENTING OURSELVES TO GOD

Extract from a sermon by Watchman Nee[1]

> ...yield yourselves unto God, as those that are alive from the dead, and your members *as* instruments of righteousness unto God (Romans 6:13, KJV).

Servant or slave?

If we give ourselves to God, many adjustments may have to be made—in [our] family, or business, or church relationships, or in the matter of our personal views. God will not let anything of ourselves remain. His finger will touch, point by point, everything that is not of Him, and will say, "This must go." Are you willing? It is foolish to resist God, and always wise to submit to Him. We admit that many of us still have controversies with the Lord. He wants something, while we want something else. Many things we dare not look into, dare not pray about, dare not even think about, lest we lose our peace. We can evade the issue in that way, but to do so will bring us out of the will of God. It is always an easy matter to get out of His will, but it is a blessed thing just to hand ourselves over to Him and let Him have His way with us.

How good it is to have the consciousness that we belong to the

[1] From *The Normal Christian Life*, 74–75. Used by kind permission.

Lord and are not our own! There is nothing more precious in the world. It is that which brings the awareness of His continual presence, and the reason is obvious. I must first have the sense of God's possession of me before I can have the sense of His presence with me. When once His ownership is established, then I dare do nothing in my own interests, for I am His exclusive property. "Know ye not, that to whom ye present yourselves as servants unto obedience, His servants ye are whom ye obey" (Romans 6:16). The word here rendered "servant" really signifies a bondservant, a slave. This word is used several times in the second half of Romans 6.

What is the difference between a servant and a slave? A servant may serve another, but the ownership does not pass to that other. If he likes his master he can serve him, but if he does not like him he can give in his notice, and seek another master. Not so is it with the slave. He is not only the servant of another, but he is the possession of another. How did I become the slave of the Lord? On His part He bought me, and on my part I presented myself to Him. By right of redemption I am God's property, but if I would be His slave I must willingly give myself to Him, for He will never compel me to do so.

The trouble with many Christians today is that they have an insufficient idea of what God is asking of them. How glibly they say, "Lord, I am willing for anything." Do you know that God is asking of you your very life? There are cherished ideals, strong wills, precious relationships, much-loved work, that will have to go; so do not give yourself to God unless you mean it. God will take you seriously, even if you do not mean it seriously.

When the Galilean boy brought his bread to the Lord, what did the Lord do with it? He broke it. God will always break what is offered to Him. He breaks what He takes, but after breaking it He blesses and uses it to meet the needs of others. After you give yourself to the Lord, He begins to break what was offered to Him. Everything seems to go wrong, and you protest and find fault with the ways of God. But to stay there is to be no more than to be just a broken vessel—no good for the world because you have gone too far for the world to use you, and no good for God either because you have not gone far enough for Him to use you. You are out of gear with the world, and you have a controversy with God. This is the tragedy of many a Christian.

My giving of myself to the Lord must be an initial fundamental act. Then, day by day, I must go on giving to Him, not finding fault with His use of me, but accepting with praise even what the flesh finds hard. That way lies true enrichment.

I am the Lord's, and now no longer reckon myself to be my own, but acknowledge in everything His ownership and authority. That is the attitude God delights in, and to maintain it is true consecration. I do not consecrate myself to be a missionary or a preacher; I consecrate myself to God to do His will where I am, be it in school, office or kitchen or wherever He may, in His wisdom, send me. Whatever He ordains for me is sure to be the very best, for nothing but good can come to those who are wholly His.

May we always be possessed by the consciousness that we are not our own.

Appendix iii

HOW TO WORSHIP GOD

A sermon by Pastor Fan Peiji[1]

> Yet a time is coming and has now come when the true worshipers will worship the Father in spirit and truth, for they are the kind of worshipers the Father seeks (John 4:23, NIV).

We should assemble together to worship the Lord every Sunday. But we must not merely observe a particular day to perform worship nor listen to some teaching. The God in whom we trust is the one and only Lord. He is the Almighty Father, the Creator of all things and rules over everything. He is omnipresent and omniscient. He is the Sovereign Lord. He is so great that the heaven is his throne and the earth is his footstool. The universe is not sufficient to contain him.

This great Sovereign Lord is also so small that he can indwell the humble and penitent heart of the person who confesses his sin and puts his trust in God. The angels and archangels around God's throne cry out to one another, "Holy, holy, holy, is the Lord of hosts." Also a blade of grass and the colourful flower show the glories of God's creation.

Hence it is a tragedy that human beings have spoilt the world

[1] Translated by Pastor David Cheung.

and turned towards evil. Every redeemed child of God should worship him in true repentance and piety.

Preparation for worship

In Old Testament times those who wanted to worship and serve God had to make careful preparation. Before Abraham offered up Isaac he arose early that morning and prepared the wood for the burnt offering. On the Day of Atonement the Passover lamb had to be killed and offered on the 14th day of the first month, but on the 10th [day] everything had to be prepared. The priest had to cleanse himself and wash his clothes before he offered the sacrifice.

When we come to the New Testament Jesus Christ has atoned for our sins, and no further sacrifice is needed; so we can approach the throne of grace without a sense of guilt. But at the same time we must come before God with reverence and fear. We should not speak to him hurriedly or casually (Ecclesiastes 5:1–2); we should not make promises we do not intend to keep. We must pray in sincerity and uprightness.

Before even we leave home for church we should pray, so that we do not shelter evil or wrong actions when we enter his house. We go to our seats in silence and prayerfulness, rather than talk noisily with others about mundane matters. We not only make sure that our clothes are clean and neat. More important it is to have a pure spirit and the cleansing of the blood of Christ. Isaiah speaks of the priests who observe all the feasts but do evil deeds "To what purpose *is* the multitude of your sacrifices unto me? ...I am full of the burnt offerings of rams ...When ye come to appear before me, who hath required this at your hand, to tread my courts?" (Isaiah 1:11–12, KJV).

The meaning of worship

From God's viewpoint we should worship him for the following reasons:

(a) To worship is to show respect to God. Nowadays we are too casual in our worship. We take too much for granted. Paul says, "Let us keep clear of anything that smirches body or soul. Let us prove our reverence for God by consecrating ourselves to Him completely" (2 Corinthians 7:1, J.B. PHILLIPS).

(b) To worship is to submit to God. When Hilkiah, the High Priest, found the book of the law in the temple he read it out to King Josiah, who on hearing these words rent his clothes and acknowledged his nation's sins. As soon as he submitted himself and humbled himself before God, God received him. We must likewise submit to God for his blessing (2 Kings 22:8–19).

(c) To worship is to love and respect. A woman who lived a sinful life knelt in front of Jesus, and wet his feet with her tears. She used her hair to dry his feet, and anointed them with perfume. This revealed the depth of her love for him. On the other hand the Pharisee was full of his own self-righteousness. This kind of worship does not please God.

The history of worship

(a) During the time of the patriarchs every tent was a place of worship. The head of the family was the priest for his household. This was true of Abraham, Isaac, Jacob and the patriarchs.

(b) In the time of Moses God was worshipped in the Tabernacle. The priest represented the people before God.

(c) In the time of King Solomon a temple was built for the worship of Jehovah God. The people worshipped God in the temple. Then the temple was destroyed and birds built their nests there. Later King Herod rebuilt it, but it became a den of thieves. Worship degenerated into mere external formality, and it was destroyed, with not one stone left on another.

(d) From the time of the New Testament period we can worship God at any time and in any place. The worship of the church is absolutely different from that of the temple. The temple of today is the temple of our human hearts, which must be kept holy for the service of God (1 Corinthians 3:16–17).

The content of our worship

(a) The singing of hymns. We must be careful not only to sing with our lips but also with our hearts, which should be filled with gratitude as we do this. The singing of hymns should move us because we are referring to our experiences. Then our spirits are brought into the third heaven.

(b) Prayer. There are many forms of prayer, which can be public, private, simultaneous with other people praying, or led by one individual. Prayer consists of connecting our spirits with God's spirit. Prayer is not only us talking to God, but him speaking to us. In our Lord's parable the Pharisee prayed so that other people would hear him, and the more he prayed the more he stood accused by God.

Listening to the sermon

Listening to the sermon is an important part of public worship. God's children should constantly receive his teaching. The Bible is our textbook. The preacher is our counsellor. The unfaithful pastor is not a true shepherd, and his preaching becomes a case of the blind leading the blind. It is important to listen carefully to the sermon, and receive the words as from the Lord. In Acts 10, Cornelius and his family came together and heard God's word as Peter proclaimed it.

The effects of worship

If we sincerely worship God we will experience his mercy as the Holy Spirit shows us who we actually are. Job responded by saying, "My ears had heard of you but now my eyes have seen you. Therefore I despise myself and repent in dust and ashes" (Job 42:5–6, NIV). Isaiah cried out, "Woe to me...I am ruined!" (Isaiah 6:5, NIV). The aged John fell at Christ's feet as if he were dead (Revelation 1:17). If we truly worship God our spiritual lives will be transformed, as with Moses and Paul.

If we truly worship God there will come to us great contentment in our hearts, as well as joy and peace. "He giveth power to the faint; and to *them that have* no might he increaseth strength. Even the youths shall faint and be weary, and the young men shall utterly fall: But they that wait upon the Lord shall renew *their* strength; they shall mount up with wings as eagles; they shall run, and not be weary; and they shall walk, and not faint" (Isaiah 40:29–31, KJV).

Appendix iv

MAP OF CHINA

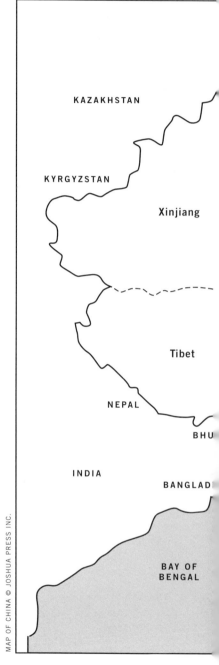

KAZAKHSTAN

KYRGYZSTAN

Xinjiang

Tibet

NEPAL

BHU

INDIA

BANGLAD

BAY OF
BENGAL

MAP OF CHINA © JOSHUA PRESS INC.

RUSSIA
MONGOLIA
Heilongjiang
Jilin
Liaoning
SEA OF JAPAN
NORTH KOREA
SOUTH KOREA
Inner Mongolia
BEIJING
Tianjin
Hebei
Ningxia
Shanxi
Shandong
inghai
YELLOW SEA
Gansu
Shaanxi
Henan
Jiangsu
Anhui
Shanghai
Hubei
Yangtze R.
Sichuan
Zhejiang
Chongqing
Jiangxi
EAST CHINA SEA
Hunan
Fujian
Guizhou
TAIWAN
Yunnan
Guangdong
Guangxi
PACIFIC OCEAN
NMAR
Hong Kong
VIETNAM
LAOS
Hainan
PHILIPPINES
THAILAND
SOUTH CHINA SEA
CAMBODIA

Sources

Chapter 1: Allen Yuan
Allen Yuan, *The Story of my Life* (Beijing, 1997).
Liang Huizhen (Mrs. Yuan), tape recording about her life, translated by Ms. Ying Ye.

Chapter 2: Esther Cui
Esther Cui, interview with author, June 18, 1997.
The Newsletter, West China Evangelistic Band.

Chapter 3: Watchman Nee
Angus I. Kinnear, *Against the Tide* (Fort Washington, Pennsylvania: Christian Literature Crusade, 1973).
N.H. Cliff, "The Life and Theology of Watchman Nee" (M.Phil. Thesis, Open University, 1983).
Watchman Nee, *My Testimony* (Booklet dated October 18, 1936, Shanghai)
"Some Facts about the Life of Watchman Nee and of his Wife," translated from *Eternal Word Magazine* (Shanghai, 1990).
Stephen Chan, *My Uncle, Nee Tuosheng,* translated from Chinese, 1968.
Deng Zhaoming, "The Waves of the Local Church," *Bridge Magazine* [Christian Study Centre on Chinese Religion and Culture, Hong Kong] (Nov./Dec. 1992; Jan./Feb. 1993).
Witness Lee, *Watchman Nee* (Anaheim, California: Living Streams, 1991).

Chapter 4: Fan Peiji
Fen Peiji, various letters to author.

Notes on the life of Fan Peiji supplied by Fan Pu, Fan Yong and Fan Sheng.

Leslie Lyall, *Three of China's Mighty Men* (London: OMF, 1973).

Chapter 5: Wu Mujia
Wu Mujia, recorded interview with author, 1990.

Wu Mujia, "My Testimony," translated by Ms. Ying Ye, printed leaflet, undated.

Leslie Lyall, *God Reigns in China* (London: Hodder and Stoughton, 1985).

G.R. Senior, *For Love of the Chinese* (Plymouth, England: E.J. Rickard, 1989).

Chapter 6: Graham Wu
Personal diary of Wu Guangya, translated by Dr. Wu Xingwang.

G.R. Senior, *The China Experience—a Study of the Methodist Church in China* (London: WMHS Publications, 1994).

J. Stanfield, *From Manchu to Mao* (London: Epworth Press, 1980).

Chapter 7: David Wang
Martin Wang, interview with author, June 10, 1998.

Mary Wang, *The Chinese Church that will not die* (London: Hodder & Stoughton, 1971).

Mary Wang, *God's School in Red China* (London: Hodder & Stoughton, 1976).

Chapter 8: Wang Zhen
Wang Aiyi, *Pastor Wang Zhen—a Life of Following the Lord*, translated by Terence Chan.

Wang Aiyi, interview with author, November 1, 1998.

Marie Stephany, *The Power of the Gospel in Shansi Province* (Springfield, Missouri: Assemblies of God, 1939).

Bibliography

BOOKS

Broomhall, A.J. *Hudson Taylor & China's Open Century*. London: Hodder & Stoughton, 1989.

Chan, Kim-Kwong and Alan Hunter. *Prayers and Thoughts of Chinese Christians*. London: Mowbray, 1991.

Chu, Moses. *The Development of Education in Chefoo*. Sondersburg, Pennsylvania: Moses Chu, 1991.

Green, Michael. *I believe in Satan's Downfall*. London: Hodder & Stoughton, 1980.

Hayward, Victor. *Christians and China*. Belfast: Christian Journals, 1974.

Hong, Silas. *The Dragon Net*. Eastbourne: Victory Press, 1976.

Kinnear, Angus I. *Against the Tide*. Fort Washington, Pennsylvania: Christian Literature Crusade, 1973.

Lee, Witness. *Watchman Nee*. California: Living Streams, 1991.

Lyall, Leslie. *God Reigns in China*. London: Hodder & Stoughton, 1985.

Lyall, Leslie. *Three of China's Mighty Men*. London: OMF, 1973.

Padilla, C. Rene. *The New Face of Evangelicalism*. London: Hodder & Stoughton, 1976.

Senior, G.R. *For Love of the Chinese*. Plymouth: E.J.Rickard, 1989.

Senior, G.R. *The China Experience—a Study of the Methodist Church in China*. London: WMHS Publications, 1994.

Stanfield, John. *From Manchu to Mao*. London: Epworth Press, 1980.

Stephany, Marie. *The Power of the Gospel in Shansi Province.* Springfield, Missouri: Assemblies of God, 1939.

Varg, Paul. *Missionaries, Chinese and Diplomats.* Princeton: Princeton University, 1958.

Wang, Mary. *The Chinese Church that will not die.* London: Hodder & Stoughton, 1971.

Wang, Mary. *God's School in Red China.* London: Hodder & Stoughton, 1976.

Wang, Mingdao. *A Stone Made Smooth.* Translated by Arthur Reynolds. Southampton: Mayflower Christian Books, 1981.

ARTICLES & BOOKLETS

Chan, Stephen. *My Uncle, Nee Tuosheng.* Translated from Chinese, 1968.

Mujia, Wu. *My Testimony.* Translated Ms. Ying Ye, printed leaflet, undated.

Nee, Watchman. *My Testimony.* Shanghai: booklet dated October 18, 1936.

"Some Facts about the Life of Watchman Nee and of his Wife" Translated from *Eternal Word Magazine*, Shanghai, 1990.

The Newsletter, West China Evangelistic Band.

Wang, Aiyi. *Pastor Wang Zhen—a Life of following the Lord.* Translated by Terence Chan.

Yuan, Allen. *The Story of my Life.* Beijing: 1997.

Zhaoming, Deng. "The Waves of the Local Church." *Bridge Magazine*, Nov./Dec. 1992; Jan./Feb. 1993.

INTERVIEWS, TAPES & LETTERS

Aiyi, Wang. Interview with author, November 1, 1998.

Cui, Esther. Interview with author, June 18, 1997.

Guangya, Wu. Personal Diary. Translated Dr. Wu Xingwang.

Huizhen, Liang (Mrs. Yuan). Tape recording about her life. Translated Ms. Ying Ye.

Mujia, Wu. Recorded interview with author, 1990.

Notes on the life of Fan Peiji supplied by Fan Pu, Fan Yong and Fan Sheng.

Peiji, Fan. Various letters to author.

Wang, Martin. Interview with author, June 10, 1998.

Deo Optimo et Maximo Gloria
To God, best and greatest, be glory

Set in Sabon
Printed in Canada

© 2001 by Joshua Press Inc.